STORIES I WI
I DIDN'T WRIIE

A COLLECTION OF EMBARRASSING MEMOIRS
BY
DAVIN DAVIS

This book is dedicated to all of you with a dream.
Chase it. Don't ever stop following it. Don't listen to people who say you
can't make it happen, especially yourself.

Special Thanks

Mom – For being my biggest fan and #1 supporter since as far back as I can remember.

Dad – For always being there for me even when I didn't want to be there for you. This book starts with you.

Adeel Siddiqui - For saving this book not once, but twice. Without Adeel, you wouldn't be reading this now. My best friend for life.

Cody "Frody" Freeman – For always pushing me to be the best version of myself even when I don't want you to. For being the positive to my pessimism.

James "Arrow" Smith – I can't think of anything. You are a terrible person.

I love you all.

Written, Poorly Edited, and Book Cover Design
by Davin Davis

Photos
by Cody Freeman and Danny Freeman,
TES Media LLC

Special thanks to Brian and Jessica McCloud for that very heavy, very cool typewriter.

Foreword

Well, here it is. Over 10 years' worth of writing. Over 34 years' worth of stories about my life. This book, the stories you're about to read, are nothing more than a thank you letter. A thank you letter to my mom who always encouraged my writing since I was very young. A thank you letter to my dad who is the center piece of a lot of the stories you're about to read. A thank you letter to every friend who encouraged me when I had no encouragement there. A thank you letter to every single person who ever wrote a comment of some form on my social media that said, "You should be a writer." There have been a lot of you. Too many to name here. It's because of these people why you're reading this.

I don't know how many of you are going to buy this book. I've had countless people tell me that if I ever wrote a book, they would buy it. Now that I've invested my time and money into this, you better keep your part of the deal. I don't want to run into you on the street and you be like, "Yeah, when I said that I was just trying to get you to buy me a beer." I'm not one of those people where I'm like, "It really doesn't matter to me, though, if it's one person or a million people who buy this book. You helped make my dream come true." Yeah, fuck that. A million people would be perfect. Honestly, I want to make enough money selling this book to where I never have to write another embarrassing story about me ever again. I'm tired of telling friends, family, and strangers about ingrown hairs on my testicles. Not that anyone is forcing me to tell these things but that's not the point.

This book is both a collection of stories I (poorly) wrote on forms of social media throughout my life (and then updated with better writing) and brand-new stories no one has ever read yet. This is a book for both old fans who supported me and for new readers who have never heard of me. I encourage people that when you're done with this book and you enjoyed it, give it to someone who has never heard my name, who has never read any of my stories. It'd be cool if you just bought them a copy, or if you send them the link to buy me a copy, but whatever. I get it.

Also, I should note, I did all the writing, all the editing on this book myself. That will become very apparent as you make your way through my life's adventures. I write the same way I talk. I don't talk in proper English, using nouns, verbs, pronouns, preposition conjunctions – whatever the hell that is. This is my voice, my message. Your job is to interpret each story however you see fit through my writings. There will be bad grammar. There will be run-on sentences. A ton of sentences that start with "And." I'm not even sure if you put the period before the quotation mark when quoting something, or after, but "whatever". Probably a couple misspellings I didn't catch. I'm not even sure I used the same font in every story, but I don't care. Ten years from now I will probably be embarrassed I ever released this to the public, but honestly, I'm tired of writing it.

You must understand why I'm tired of writing it. This is absolutely true: I have lost this book twice now. When I decided to write this book, I began collecting old stories from my social media accounts from Xanga, Myspace, and Facebook and saving them to a computer. Eventually, once I had enough collected, I was going to publish this book. The first computer I saved them on crapped out on me out of nowhere. Literally, I came home one day, went to turn the computer on, and it just never turned back on. I got the hard drive out of the computer and hooked it up to a new computer and when I did, I discovered most of the files on the hard drive were lost and corrupted. So many stories, gone forever. I was absolutely devastated. It felt like I had the air punched out of me and almost told myself, "Maybe this is just a sign you shouldn't write a book." But as I continued to write blogs on social media, I got the bug all over again. People would consistently say, "You need to be a writer."

So, I had to start all over. The second time I tried to write this book, I had saved and written every single story that you're about to read onto a laptop. One day, because I'm a dumbass, I left that laptop in the back seat of my car with the window down and on that same day, it rained. It rained hard. When I found my laptop, it was dripping from the inside with water. As you can imagine, the computer was completely ruined.

Once again, I was deflated, but became determined. I was smarter this time, as I had saved all of my stories on backups. Unfortunately, I didn't save ALL of them completed. This will be my third, and possibly, final attempt to get this out to you guys. I don't think I can suffer through this again.

Also, every time I read and re-read this thing, I see punchlines I could punch up. Make better, at least in my head. I'm scared that if I think too much, criticize myself too much, the stories that were once good will now be trash. So, this is it. This is basically me in a small bathroom reader you'll most likely keep on the back of your toilet. That will be my legacy.

Thank you for buying. Thank you for reading. Thank you for sharing. Thank you for encouraging. I hope it's not, but even if this is the last book I ever write, I just want you to know as you're reading it, I am the happiest I have ever been.

Now here's way too much information about me that's about to be burned into your brain forever.

Enjoy. Let's get this over with.

LAWNMOWER BOMB

There are a few stories in this book about my father, but this is my absolute favorite. We have told this story at nearly every Thanksgiving and Christmas, and it still kills every here.

We were living in Missouri and my family had bought this A&W restaurant that had a house connected to it. Behind the house was this wide parking lot for customers and behind that, there was this huge back yard. Now it's important to point out Dad wasn't exactly known for his patience. Saying he had a bit of a temper would be an understatement. So, this one time he tells my brothers, during the middle of a lunch shift, "Get out there and mow that back yard."

My brothers, EJ and Jason, go out back with the lawnmower and try to crank it. It doesn't crank. Tries again. Doesn't crank. They try, try, try and this damn lawnmower just isn't cranking. They go inside and tell Dad, "The lawnmower isn't starting." My Dad, being who he is, just flies off the handle, which was typical in our house. "You're all just a bunch of a lazy motherfuckers, just don't want to mow the fucking grass," even though they legitimately tried to turn on the lawnmower. That's just Dad.

Dad pulls the lawnmower onto the back parking lot right behind the restaurant. He tries to crank it. Nothing happens. Cranks it again. Nothing happens. Cranks. Cranks. Cranks. Now Dad is cussing God and anybody in his line of vision about the lawnmower as my brothers are standing there with this proud, "See, it's not working" smirk on their face.

You have to understand, my father is a very stubborn man. I once heard a story where he kept getting shocked repeatedly trying to repair an eggbeater machine at Waffle House. Customers could hear him in the back: *BZZZZZ* "Damn it!" A few seconds later, *BZZZZ* "God damn it," as the lights flickered in the restaurant. So, if a few extremely dangerous shocks of electricity couldn't stop him, this lawnmower didn't stand a chance.

Dad, bound and determined, grabs that lawnmower handle with one hand, grabs the cord with his other hand like he's about to pull Excalibur from its stone, and yanks it as hard as he can.

The good news was the lawnmower started.

The bad news was it immediately engulfed itself in fire. Six-foot-high flames shot up in the middle of the parking lot during a lunch shift. Black smoke filling the backlot. The lawnmower was on fire!

So, my dad's natural reaction is to push it away from him and the kids in case it explodes, right? Well, when he pushes it, it starts rolling down the parking lot towards a customer's vehicle. Now, working in the restaurant industry for over 15 years, I've been in multiple situations where I have had to apologize to customers. I cannot imagine having to explain to a customer, "Well our lawn mower caught on fire, and we maybe kind of accidentally pushed it towards your vehicle and it caused significant damage. So, here's a coupon for a free chips and salsa. You're welcome."

The lawnmower is on fire slowly rolling down this parking lot as a look of terror and confusion is written all over Dad's face. I mean, what do you do in that situation? On one hand, if you don't grab the lawnmower, there is a chance it could explode, or you could get badly burned. On the other hand, it could roll into a customer's car, causing damage. We could get sued. The lawnmower fire could cause fire to a car, and next thing you know there's a domino effect of fire cars exploding in our parking lot.

Dad screams, "Someone get some water!" My brother Jason runs into the house as there's chaos and panic happening in the parking lot. Dad is yelling at EJ as if this is his fault somehow, all while there are customers inside who have no idea what is going on. Just eating their meals not knowing there is a firebomb just a couple yards away from their table. I can just see a customer enjoying a nice relaxing burger after a hard day at work listening to the jukebox, and in the background Dad and EJ are chasing a burning lawnmower across the parking lot.

Jason, responding to Dad's orders to get water, comes running out of the house with a CUP, a CUP, of water. When Jason finally gets to the lawnmower, he starts running sideways along the side of it because it's still rolling, and as he does, the water is spilling out of his small cup. So much water spilled out by the time he decides to throw it, there's less than half of the water remaining. He throws his pathetic glass of water onto the mower and all it did was just disappear into the fire. I think it evaporated before it even hit the mower.

Dad grabbed the lawnmower by the handles, turned it, and pushed it into the backward before it struck any customer's card. Him, EJ, and Jason just stood there on the edge of the parking lot watching it burn, hoping it wouldn't catch the grass on fire.

Eventually, the fire died, and the lawnmower was now a smoking, charred mess of its former self. Customers leaving the restaurant would walk to their car and see the three of them staring at this pile of fire in the backyard. And Dad had to put on that stupid restaurant voice in front of customers, even though he was lava-hot angry, when they ask, "What happened?"

"Oh, you know! Another day, another dollar. Fire is crazy, right? Did you enjoy your meal?"

Luckily, the lawnmower didn't explode, no one got hurt, and no cars were hit.

Unfortunately, though, the grass still needed to be mowed.

-*Written for Dad on Father's Day 2016.*

DAD CUSSES OUT A CHURCH

My father once cussed out an entire church softball team that had special needs players.

You are intrigued already. More on that in a bit.

This story happened in the Summer of 1995 in the quiet little town of Willow Springs, Missouri. My family had just purchased an A&W restaurant and my father had plans to move his entire family and extended family and run this A&W fast food restaurant as a family business. It was my father, my mother, my sister, my two brothers, my two brother's friends, their girlfriends, my brother's girlfriends. There may have been people living there I don't even remember, there were so many of us. My dad made it work though. He built walls in almost every room of the house to divide the space so everyone could have their own room. It was pretty cool actually how he turned that little home into an apartment building. That was probably the last time my family was happy living there, the first day. The entire story of my family living in Willow Springs could be a book of its own, but this isn't the place to talk about kidnappings and multiple attempted murders. Let's keep it fun!

When we moved to town, we found this other little hole-in-the-wall restaurant called North Café. It was owned by a man named Chris North and his titan-like wife and children. They were a big family, in every direction. At least I remember them being that way. I was just a twelve-year-old kid, but I remember North's teenage boys being giant assholes with giant assholes. They once purposely flipped me off their trampoline by jumping down at the same time. They were pushing the trampoline down as I was coming down so when I hit, the trampoline rocketed me into the air. I thought I had become an X-Man in that moment. Like I had just discovered my power of flight, I was so high in the air. Unfortunately, that was not true as they jettisoned me off the trampoline, I lost my flight ability and I landed on top of my neck and shoulders on the unforgiving ground. My neck hurt for days after that. They literally could have killed me. But I did my job because I've always enjoyed making people laugh and they seemed to have a very good chuckle laughing on the trampoline as I unfolded myself from my pretzel-like form.

One fateful day as these things happen, Chris, in a classy move, had invited us to his restaurant to congratulate us on owning the A&W restaurant and mentioned to my father that he had a softball team that played against other business's softball teams. Chris and his two Walrus-like sons played on the team. My father's ears perked. It was a mistake Chris had not known he had made. He had just shown a Ribeye steak to a starving wolf. My father told Chris that he too enjoyed a gentleman's game of softball and that his boys, my brothers, played quite well. What my dad was trying to tell Chris is, "My team doesn't leave the field until everyone is bleeding."

You must understand something about my father. My father has always been, as far back as I can remember, a very competitive person. I don't mean he gets angry when he loses. No, no silly goose. I mean he will insult your grandmother's sex life over a game of Monopoly and I'm talking about my grandmother. He has hurt the feelings of many family members during Life, both the board game and reality. When you grow up with a father like that, you just get used to it. It becomes normal. "Yeah, my dad threatened to beat a six-year-old with a baseball bat if he didn't 'move his ass' around third base. What's your point?" When you play sports with Dad, welcome to No Fun Land. Meet the Mayor, Emotional Trauma and Unsportsmanlike Conduct

When Chris heard about my dad also enjoying a friendly game of softball, he invited my dad to be the assistant coach of the team. Little did he know in my dad's head, he's not assistant anything. He's the coach now. As far as Dad was concerned, he had formed this team from the beginning and invented softball. Coach Dad, deal with it. And they did. The town, the family, innocent players and bystanders all dealt with it.

My father had been the coach of a lot of business teams over the years. When I was about eight years old, he was the District Manager of Waffle House and he had formed a basketball team with him, his family, and some employees who did not know what they had done. The colors of the Waffle House logo are black and yellow, so he had someone make airbrushed black t-shirts with yellow paint for them to wear on the court like jerseys. Everyone had the stupidest nicknames you've ever heard airbrushed on the back. Things like "Dunkin' Davis," who was my father. "Dribbling Davis" who was my brother. "Piece of shit who can't make a simple layup Davis" was my less-talented brother. "Slamming Steve" who was my dad's boss.

One time they were scheduled to play against the local police department, but the police department decided to pull a fast one and instead of my dad and family playing the cops, they were now playing the inmates. Inmates. Seven-foot five violent criminals. These young bloods hit the court and were dunking the ball like rabid Michael Jordans. Doing these incredible passes and maneuvers as my dad's team looked on in horror.

The announcer announced each team and by words alone, it looked like it was going to be a bloodbath.

"Coming down the court at 5'11, Dunkin Davis!"

"And their opponents, from the isolated cell blocks of Monroe, Louisiana State Penitentiary, weighing in at 275 lbs. and standing at 6 feet 9 inches, from parts unknown, Louisiana, with three felonies and two misdemeanors, T-Dogg Jenkins!"

It had to have been the most lop-sided game in sports history. Even then, my dad got angry at his teammates. "What the hell? How you gonna let that refrigerator of a man dunk on you? Are you even trying?" Like my dad was just hitting threes and doing layups all day around these guys. He contributed just about as much as any other loser on the court that day.

That was child's play compared to the, we'll call it the *incident*, that happened when my dad's A&W softball team (formerly known as the North Café softball team) took on the Pomona Christian Church softball team. Pomona is the name of a town in Missouri and after a quick Google search, it seems their Church is still going strong. Nice looking church. Just in case any member of the Pomona Christian Church is reading this, or anyone who has a special needs member in their family, I would like to apologize for what you are about to read.

About three innings into the game the sanity strings in my dad's brain were slowly unraveling. Here he is, the man who would insult his own mother for not hitting a home run, having to restrain himself as he is playing against a Christian-owned team with special needs players. He probably gave himself a hernia holding in what can only be described as a stern prison vocabulary. There's Christian members sitting in the audience bleachers. There's Christian players. Our own teammates were Christian, and then there's Dad, who *claimed* to be Christian.

People began noticing Dad slowly unraveling when he was giving encouraging advice to his teammates such as, "You guys are playing like a bunch of fucking morons!" You know, that healthy, athletic spirit. "Get your head out of your ass," he would yell with uplifting motivation to my older brother. My father is belittling his entire team in front of the Lord's people. A shush would fall over the audience as parents began putting their hands over their child's ears. I half expected the audience to start singing hymns to blockade the evil demons spewing from my dad's mouth. "We must sacrifice a virgin to cleanse our souls of this man's words of hatred and disgust."

To my dad, if he made you cry during a game, your tears meant he was doing his job right. A broken spirit meant you played a good game.

The insults kept coming throughout the entire game. My father was a big, tough, intimidating man so not many people wanted to exchange words or blows with him. Not that that would have mattered anyway because insulting someone was just Dad's way of motivation and defamation. Two for the price of one. It finally escalated when Dad let all the rage out. He said the line that is forever echoed every Thanksgiving and every Christmas when we tell this story. The line that will live in infamy. My father looks around at the scoreboard, turns back and looks across the field to his team, and says...

"You're being beaten by a bunch of fucking retards!"

I know, hurt reader. I know. I understand the calamity of that statement. I am not telling this story to insult you or your loved ones, but it was said, loudly, clearly, and the hard R of "ards" echoed off the bleachers back to the scoreboard, and back again.

"Ards... ards... ards..."

Pigeons screamed and flew off into the night. That was it. Insult your teammates and children all day long, sure. But once you start using slurs like that in front of handicapped people, that was it. The umpire of the game finally had enough and banished my dad to the "dugout" which was just a small fenced in area for the players to sit. The umpire might as well as given my dad a megaphone because the insults just got louder.

"Ah goddammit, you can't hit shit," he screamed to a crying grown man on home plate with two strikes. He even began talking loudly to himself. "I swear if he doesn't hit this ball, I'm going to beat him with his own baseball glove." He just kept going and going. The umpire finally paused the game and kicked my dad out of the dugout. My father has now basically been kicked out of the game twice. You think that calmed things down? My dad is now behind the fence walking towards the bleachers. "I'm going to join this church just so I can play for a winning team!" I don't think they'll accept you Dad. Any reasonable human being might have taken the hint but not Dad. He actually goes and stands in the bleachers with the audience and shouting "advice" to his team, in the way that if Yosemite Sam with Tourette's syndrome was giving advice.

His advice didn't work as the A&W team lost to Pomona Christian Church 8 – 2. Oof. That had to have been the most awkward post-game handshake ever. My family apologizing to the other team and the other team rubbing holy water on the A&W team. I bet my dad was the subject of an entire sermon the following Sunday. The preacher on stage probably said something like, "People, I can confirm there are demons among us who preach the gospel of Satan."

There were still four games left in the season to go. Heaven help them.

CAMPING IS FOR SOCIOPATHS

So, I may or may not be a part of a few dating sites. And by a few, I mean everyone you can think of. Eharmony, PlentyOfFish, OkCupid, HumanTraffickingLove, all the popular ones, and there's two things I look at in every profile I visit. First, I look at the pictures to see what the cash and prizes look like, cause I'm shallow, and then I look for the word "camping". Because I've noticed something on *a lot* of profiles. There are, apparently, tons of people who enjoy going camping. And when I see the word "camping" I swipe left, or whatever you kids are calling it these days. Basically, I'm like "nope" and move on. Because when I see the word camping, I see the words "lying liar lying through your lying hole."

Nobody should ever enjoy camping. No one, besides maybe Bear Grylls. I've been camping twice in my life and both times were horrible. It was borderline horror movie. I think when people say they enjoy camping, to quote Inigo Montoya from The Princess Bride, "I do not think it means what you think it means." I think when these people hear the word "camping" they think, "Hey, my rich uncle has a two-story cabin near the lake with cabinets filled with liquor and a built-in hot tub. If we get bored, we can go on the jet ski." That's not the kind of camping I'm talking about. I mean *real* camping.

Imagine trying to invite someone to go camping with you and they have no idea what camping was. If you described it to them, you would sound like a sociopath. You would. The conversation would go like...

"Hey, you wanna go camping this weekend?"

"Camping? What's that?"

"It's where we spend one or two nights in the middle of the forest."

"...In the forest? Are we staying in a house in the forest?"

"No, we'll be sleeping on the forest floor with the ticks, spiders, and snakes."

"Sleeping on the forest floor? Well will we at least have some type of shelter from protection from the bugs or in case the weather gets bad?"

"Yeah, we'll be protected by this thing called a tent which is about as thin as your t-shirt and catches wind like the sail on a ship."

"What?! Well, what if a bear or mountain lion comes along?"

"Oh, don't worry about that. All we must do is tie our food really high to a tree, so the bears won't eat it. And hopefully the ants won't find it either."

"Ants?! Bears and ants are trying to eat our food and we have to tie it to a tree? Well, is there anything to do that is relaxing? Can we swim in a pond or lake or something?"

"Yeah, we could but we need to be careful because the lake is where all the mosquitoes, leeches, and broken glass are?"

"Wait, wait! Hold on? You want me to go in the middle of the forest, at night, where ticks, spiders, snakes, mosquitoes, leeches, broken glass, bears, and possibly mountain lions are constantly trying to eat us or our food? And the only thing protecting us against all of it is a tent?"

"Yes, and don't forget ants."

"Uh... well can I at least bring my cell phone so, in case of an emergency, I can call someone?

"Yeah, you could but getting service out in the middle of the forest is really hard."

You see where I'm going with this. It only gets worst if you think about it. And let's not even forget about the crystal meth tweakers who have a buried stash of needles next to your camp site, or the biker rapists who drink beer and throw their bottles into the lake, hints that's how the lake got broken glass in it. Also, every sound you hear that's not yours is either a hungry animal or Jason Vorhees about to cut your skull in half with his trusted machete. At least that's what you think it is.

My entire family (13 of us) went camping once in Missouri and pretty much from start to finish it was a nightmare. We found this site where people could go camp. Not log cabin camping, not air conditioner camping, I mean sleeping in the jungle heat next to a pile of deer shit camping. This will be a good idea, right? What could possibly go wrong?

Everything.

We started the day off on a horse trail. You could rent out these horses from the campground and kind of go exploring on this two-mile trail. When we got there, they told us "Well, there are 13 of you. We only have 12 horses." Then one of the workers pointed to me and said "Well, maybe he could ride Sassy." I'm not even sure if its name was Sassy but it sounds right. Sassy was the newest and youngest horse in training. Sassy did have some experience but was still new. And my family without thinking of my safety said "GIDDYUP! Let's do this." So, we start down this trail, and everything is fine at first.

And then we arrived at the lake.

All the other horses walked across this tiny, shallow lake just fine. No problem. I mean, the water was so shallow there were tiny rocks sticking out of the water. My horse, Sassy, stopped at the very edge of the shore and in horse-talk said "Psssh, fuck that. I ain't going." My entire family is on the other side of lake staring at me like I'm the asshole, because my untrained horse I was forced on was scared of the shallow water. So, my dad gets off his horse, grabs its reigns, and starts walking back over to my side of the lake. He grabs my horse by its reigns and tries to pull it into the water. Sassy didn't like that. She starts bobbing her head up and down really fast, almost head butting me in the process while her whip-like horsehair kept swiping my eyes and face, and she refuses to cross the water. Then my dad starts yelling at me because MY horse who, I apparently trained and was now trying to kill me, wouldn't cross the river. My horse is yelling at my dad. My dad is yelling at me. I'm crying because either the horse or my father is going to kill me. And my dad's horse is calmly drinking water like this situation was an everyday occurrence for it. Finally, my dad and I think one or two family members said "screw it, we'll just go back the way we came. You guys continue on the trail, and we'll meet back up."

My dad was yelling and cussing at me all the way back to the ranch. Didn't say one word to the workers who gave me the horse. Said plenty of words to me.

Fast forward to day two and my family decides "Hey, those clouds are looking pretty dark, we should go canoeing." That's not entirely true. We had already booked the canoeing down the river, but on the morning we arrived, there was no blue sky. Just gray clouds as far as the eye could see. But instead of canceling going canoeing down a, normally, peaceful river, my family said "GIDDYUP!" and off we went. Almost from the moment we all hit the water, it starts raining. But who cares right? It's just water touching more water, how bad could it be? Bad, very bad. Let me see if I can recap all the major plot points of that canoe trip.

My sister-in-law-at-the-time dropped her baby Jordan Davis into the water, which was now, not calm, but had become rapids. Thankfully, someone got him out. The river was going so fast that my other sister-in-law's canoe had smashed sideways and bent into a rock in the middle of the rapids. She and everyone else fell out and they lost everything that was not attached to their body. Beer, food, jewelry, paddles, life vests, all down the river. Luckily some strangers happened to be nearby and picked them up before the water killed them. When my dad's canoe tried to save my brothers-in-law's canoe, it too tipped over and both canoes sailed away into the night. Keep in mind, it is pouring down rain the entire time this is happening. The universe was mocking my family that day because I shit you not, by the time we finally made it to the end and everyone got out of the death canoes, it stopped raining. I believe we had to pay for the canoes and paddles that were now lost in the abyss of the rapids.

It's not over.

Everyone gets back to our camp site. Everyone is tired, worn out, wet, fighting over towels, everyone has had enough of this shit. Screw the forest, take me back to my warm, dry technology. Most of that time my memory of what happened next is lost, but what I do remember is waking up in the tent in a huge puddle of water. That's right, it started raining again, hard, and rained so bad that our tent, which was on an embankment, had flooded, and soaked through the tent. I was in a sleeping bag, in a puddle of water. The reason why I woke up, besides being cold with no sign of warmth in sight, was my family was discussing loudly (because of the pouring rain) should we stay, or should we go?

We packed up all of our stuff in the middle of the rainstorm, besides our big ass tents, I think. I remember leaving those behind, because we knew we were would never use those motherfuckers again and took off in the middle of the night during a rainstorm just so we could go back home and look at something that wasn't wet. My dad was soooooooooo pisssssssed. He spent money on 13 of us to go camping. Bought all this camping equipment that became useless and abandoned. Had to pay for damaged canoes and lost paddles. Almost got killed by a baby horse. And we never saw a dry moment.

So yeah, I said all that to say, if you enjoy going camping, you are a liar, and we shouldn't be together.

A NIGHT ON BOURBON STREET

The Backstory: In April of 2001, me and six friends from High School decided to travel to the seedy and sordid streets of New Orleans, Louisiana to encounter the Mardi Gras experience of Bourbon Street. I would like to set a disclaimer to the friends, family, employers, wives, future wives, future employers, future children of all who are involved in this story, do not judge us by the color of this story but by content of our character. I think Martin Luther King said that. We were young, stupid, underage, and had one of the best nights of our lives.

Ah, Bourbon Street. You've probably heard of this mystical and magical land at some point in your life. Some of you reading this might have been there and have your own stories you can't share for legal reasons. Bourbon Street is where the young and impressionable go to look for sex and alcohol and where the homeless are not hard to find. This story happened my senior year of high school. Six friends and I decided, for whatever forgetful reason, that we were going to Bourbon Street while being underage and had never experienced the sites we would soon see. We loaded up two cars, full of beads and a dream of seeing female boobs, and drove from Pearl, Mississippi to New Orleans, Louisiana.

Now I should prelude this story by saying several chunks of the story will be missing and several details will be foggy for obvious reasons. Well, alcohol. Alcohol is the reason. To say we got drunk would be an understatement. So, who are "we?" Shortly after graduation, a group of my friends, Wiebe, Michael, Kristen, her boyfriend Matt, Jamie, and her boyfriend, who I honestly don't remember his name because we only hung out that one time and the whole drunk thing, all decided to go to Bourbon Street. Two couples, three single guys. I remember the drive there being enjoyable. The couples were in one car. Wiebe, Michael and I were in another car talking on the way there about all the potential things that could happen. Would we see boobs? Of course. Would we try heroin? Maybe. Who knows? Don't be a pussy, bro. The drive from my then-hometown of Pearl, Mississippi to New Orleans was a little under three hours. Not a bad drive to take.

By the time we arrived in Louisiana, the sun had vanished behind the skyline. It was all fun and dreams on the drive there but when we finally arrived on the first night, nerves began to sit in. We had gotten lost. This, young children, were the days before GPS. We had to rely on a road atlas, maps, and strangely vivid directions from our parents. We found ourselves in the ghettos of Louisiana. The homeless were abundant and shady individuals stared at three white boys in a car with a Mississippi license plate like lions hunting their prey. The further we drove, the more off-putting our surroundings became. Buildings and dumpsters labeled with untalented graffiti. Heavily bearded men pushing shopping carts full of garbage bags down the sidewalk. At the time, I wasn't sure what a "hood" was but I'm pretty sure we were right in the middle of one. You could hear the nervousness in our voice as we described our surroundings.

"Hey look, that dude pissing on a dumpster is yelling at our car. Ha. That's weird." I was sure a stabbing with a shank made from a spoon was going to be involved in our future. We stopped paying attention to street names too as they were getting unnerving. Malcom X Drive. You're Not Welcome Here Avenue. Shawshank Rape Street. That is what it felt like at least. The nervousness soon turned to frustration. "Why can't we find this place?! It's the busiest, craziest, most chaotic street in America right now? And we can't find it. This is bullshit!" Minutes felt like hours. We drove, and drove, and drove until we finally turned a corner and... there it was.

It was like the Wizard of Oz going from black and white to color. We found it. We could tell we found it. There it was in all its glory. Our Oz. Our Nirvana. Bourbon Street. Neon lights filled the dark alley ways. Loud party music echoed off the buildings. Beads hung off the necks of the youth like Mr. T's gold chains. I wonder if the Angels who visited Sodom and Gomorrah in the Bible had the same feeling we did. There was a strange odor in the air that must've been a mix of vomit, beer, urine, and shame. We purposely booked our hotel near Bourbon Street and as soon as we found it, we wanted to check into our rooms and head straight to debauchery. We parked our car, checked in, and Wiebe, Michael, and I met up with the couples in the lobby and headed to the motherland.

Being from a small, football, country town in Mississippi, I was culture shocked as to what I was seeing. It seemed like thousands of drunk people were just partying right in the middle of the street. I'm staring at all the neon lights, clubs, and bars in shock and awe. Every few seconds something incredible would happen. I just saw four boobs. There's a guy being arrested screaming "Mardi Gras rules!" Is that...is that Dad? As the nervousness and frustration died down, we were standing on a sidewalk not really knowing what to do next. No one had direction. I don't think anybody wanted to be the leader of the night as far as deciding what to do and where to go. After a few minutes of standing and staring, Wiebe, Michael, and I collectively decided, "Why don't we let the couples do couple-things (whatever that is on Bourbon Street) and we'll go do single guy things," and so we did.

Here we are, The Three Underage Amigos, ready to have the night of our lives. But how? How are we going to get into bars and clubs? How are we going to get alcohol? But hey, how hard is it to acquire alcohol illegally on Bourbon Street? Turns out, not that hard at all, unless of course you are a young reader enjoying this book. Then it's extremely hard. Don't sue me, parents. We had heard that many of the clubs on Bourbon Street didn't ID. Of course, it should be noted that we heard this from kids our age who went to our high school. They probably have never even been to Bourbon Street, just trying to seem cool, and giving us false, suck ass information. Regardless, we took our chance. Across the street we saw a club with wide open doors with girls dancing in cages. That was it. That was the first club I wanted to go into.

"That one. I want that one," I said like a child seeing the biggest present under the Christmas tree. This was it. This was the moment of truth. This moment could make or break our spirits for the rest of the night. If we walk in and they ID our obvious underage licenses, they could confiscate them, call the police, maybe even blackball us. Or worst yet, they could call our parents. Michael, Wiebe, and I all give each other an unsettling nod and we walk straight in. There was five seconds of anxiety and then... nobody approached us. Not even a hint of a security system for minors at this place. We did it! We made it! Sex is in our future, our adolescent minds thought. Not two minutes after entering, this sexy, black-haired, pale-skinned, tattooed goddess walks up to the three of us.

"Hey guys, you want to do body shots with me? Only three dollars." As soon as she said "bod-", I said "Yes, please. Thank you for the suggestion. What a neighborly thing to do." She has on this Batman-like utility belt full of tubes of colorful liquor. She reaches into her belt, pulls out a tube of liquor, uncaps it, sticks it between her breasts, and says, "Who's first?" I almost facepalmed Wiebe and Michael out of the way. I put my mouth on the tube, pull back and take my shot. It was like tasting the wine of the gods on Mount Olympus. She then pulls out second liquor tube from her utility belt. Always prepared, just like Batman. She unbuttons the front of her pants a little to show us the red G-string she is wearing, sticks the tube down front of her pants, and again says, "Who's next?" Now, see, that's not fair because I didn't know vagina shots were an option. Not that I'm complaining with what I did get but still. Wiebe gets on his knees, puts the tube in his mouth, and takes the shot. I'm so jealous. She then reaches into her Batman liquor belt, pulls out a third tube, turns around, pulls her pants down just a little, sticks the tube between her ass cheeks. Michael gets the ass shot. Again, this was back before you ate the booty like groceries, or whatever the kids say nowadays. But dayumm, what an ass she had. Although all that's going through my mind at that second was "New Orleans fecal matter shot? No thank you to that."

Here's where it gets bad.

She buttons up her pants and the tone in her voice completely changes.

"Okay, that'll be eighteen dollars."

We all kind of scowled our faces and shook our heads. Wiebe was the first to say out loud what we were all thinking. "Eighteen dollars? You said they were three dollars a shot. How is it eighteen dollars?" She says, "Yeah, three dollars a shot but you were all involved with each shot. Three times nine is eighteen." Her math didn't even add up. We all looked at each other and collectively decided not to correct her terrible math. Three times nine is twenty-seven but whatever, we weren't going to argue with her math skills at that moment. Basically, she was saying because we all watched each other take each other's shots, we were paying for the privilege to watch my friend stick his nose in this girl's ass. There was a "watcher's fee," if you will, like some sort of back-alley porno being filmed. So, I say, "Um, nooo. We just watched, we didn't touch you, so it should be nine dollars total." She replies, "Well, if there's a problem, we can just get the bouncer involved." Now here we are. Three underage dudes that have just been swerved by a goth goddess. We could've ruined our night if we didn't pay the money. Possibly got our asses kicked by a bouncer. In hindsight, we were still by the doors when all this was happening, so we could've just ran out and scattered like cockroaches. What was she going to do? Chase us down the crowded street? Alas, we gave her the money. She smirks her mischievous smile and walks away. There was a brief second of anger before we just shrugged our shoulders and left the club. New Orleans - 1. Us - 0. We exited the club defeated and walked back out onto the busy street, each of us basically saying, "What a bitch!... But damn, she was hot!"

Our friend Matt told us before we got to Louisiana, "You've got to try this drink. It's called a Hand Grenade. It's super alcoholic but tastes amazing." So now that we've already had a taste of titty and ass alcohol, that was our next mission, should we choose to accept it. We had to find these Hand Grenades. Even though our very first experience on Bourbon Street was a swerve, we were still in good spirits. We had the Katt Williams' attitude: "Tonight, we're getting fucked up!" Unbeknownst to us, we were a little spoiled when we walked into that first club because the next few tries did not go so well. We tried to walk into another club a few buildings down and they ID us. We tried another club, again, they ID us. Dammit. We can't get into any clubs, so how the hell are we going to get our hands on some Hand Grenades? So, I brilliantly suggested, "Why don't we just ask somebody to buy it for us?" Not the best strategy because we are on the busiest street in the world right now surrounded by cops. But fuck it, Y.O.L.O.

I turn around and the first person walking my direction is a black lady, followed by her Mexican boyfriend. She walks by and I said, "Excuse me miss, would you buy us some drinks?" Looking back, I must've sounded like the whitest narc you've ever heard. Before she could answer, her Mexican boyfriend walks by me, puts the back of his hand on my chest and says, "Keep stepping, motherfucker" followed by a death glare. His face tattoos told me I should probably do just that, keep stepping, and that's what I did. Frustration had returned. We're underage on Bourbon Street. We have been ripped-off by a bar rat who I'm not even sure worked there at this point. Denied access to club after club after club. Threatened by a Mexican cholo. "I wonder what the couples are doing," I thought sadly. Probably drinking hand grenades in the middle of a cocaine orgy. We had no idea where they were, and we were almost at a stopping point. "Well, I guess we'll just walk the streets and polish off any empty beer bottles we find in trash cans. Hopefully nobody used them for ash trays or toilets." It was not going well. And then, like the cavalry arriving in the wild West, we turn the corner, and we see them.

Frat boys.

You could smell their names from here: Chad. Kyle. Bryson. Could these khaki shorts and pink polo shirts be our saving grace? Only one way to find out. They were all smiles, all party, and seemed like they already had a few cocktails under their belt. We walk up to one of them with a blonde frohawk (I just knew that was the guy) and said, "Look man, we want some alcohol. Specifically, Hand Grenades. If you buy them for us, we will pay for them and give you forty bucks?" His smile slowly left his face as curiosity took it over. He stares us down for a second and goes, "Are you with cops? Because if I ask you, you have to tell me."

Life hack kids: no, we don't. If the cops were to hire us for sting operations such as this, we don't have to tell you that we work with cops. That's not how the law works.

Wiebe says, "No man. We can't get into any clubs. We're just here trying to have a good time at Mardi Gras like you guys, but we wanna drink and have some fun and nobody will buy for us. Please hook us up." Wiebe, Michael and I all did drama theater in high school together. To this day, I don't know if Wiebe was acting or sounded extremely sincere but the tone in his voice sold it great. This dude hears the sympathy in Wiebe's voice and says, "Alright, three hand grenades? I'll be right back." We start pulling out our wallets and by the time we look up, he was gone. He walked away and vanished into the crowded street. We weren't even sure if he was coming back so we just stood there like a couple of assholes. But within two minutes, he returns with three neon green, long tubes with giant straws. At the bottom of those neon green tubes were the shape of hand grenades. It was beautiful. This guy was our Willy Wonka if Willy Wonka distributed liquor to minors. He passes them out to us and, in one of the coolest meeting-a-stranger moments of my life, he says, "Drinks are on me boys! Don't worry about the tip, you guys have good night." And just walks away. We were so happy in that moment. We waved goodbye to the Frat Boys like we were about to sail away on the Titanic. "Thanks guys! You guys' rule! Wooooo!"

Now, here's where the memory starts to fail, because let me tell you something about Hand Grenades. I have, since, had much liquor involved in my life but Hand Grenades are mind erasers. They are more mind erasers than the shot, mind eraser. If you want to get blackout drunk off just one drink, have yourself a Hand Grenade. Or two, like us.

The first thing I remember after getting the Hand Grenade was walking up to a liquor booth holding our empty hand Grenades and we just asked the guy if we could get another. Because we were already holding some, he didn't bother to ID us. Score! The night is already better. Like I said, things got blurry after that but here's one of the best moments of the night I do remember: The streets were crowded, and Michael and I had accidentally wandered into the middle of a circle of people staring at a balcony and yelling. We were confused at first until we look up at the balcony and there's at least ten smoking hot college girls covered in beads. I mean *covered*. Their neck, their waist, their wrist. They looked like the Michelin Man if the Michelin Man was made out of beads instead of tires. The crowd started chanting the infamous chant you hear most in New Orleans: "Show your tits! Show your tits!" Michael and I were chanting that shit like they were our football team at the Super Bowl. The girls lift their shirts, and the crowd erupts. This colorful shrapnel of beads blasts into the air like it was shot from a t-shirt gun. Okay, the exchange for goods and services is over. They showed us the cash and prizes. We throw them the beads. End of transaction, right? Wrong.

Michael and I were standing in the middle of the circle on the street, the girls looked directly at us, pointed at us, and started chanting, "Show your dick! Show your dick!" Now, I want to remind my parents, friends, and family that I was very drunk when this was happened. Young and stupid. In a moment of brilliant friendship, Michael and I look at each other, said nothing, and with our eyes and facial expressions told each other, "Should we? Let's do it!" We unbutton and at the same time whipped 'em out. I've heard rappers talking about making it rain on a stripper, but these girls made it rain on us. We were being showered with beads like a heavy rainstorm. Greatest moment of my life until one necklace simultaneously hit me in the eye and got into my mouth. I was sure of it: I now had New Orleans herpes. It had a very, shall we say, unnatural taste to it. Still, I didn't care.

Now, remember how I said earlier that the streets were surrounded by cops? Well, I zip up, turn around to high-five Michael, and behind him, walking towards us, I see a cop. Uh oh. A female cop. And she looked pissed. She walks right up to us and says, "Did you just do what I think you did?" I quickly blurt out, "Nope." She says, "Well that's good, because if you did do what I think you just did, you would be going to jail right now. And if you do it again, what I think you did, tonight, you *will* be going to jail. You're not going to make me think that again, are you?" Again, I say, "Nope." She says "Ok, walk on. Have yourself a safe night." Thank you, Officer. Could you imagine the cellmates you would have spent the night with on Mardi Gras weekend?

Memories began to fade in and out after that. I do remember some poor bastard in khaki pants standing in the middle of street, drunker than hell, pissing his pants. You could see the urine slowly soaking through his crotch to his thighs. His friends, or at least the crowd around him, were laughing their ass off, like good friends do when you piss yourself in the middle of one of the busiest streets in America. That was kind of a reality check for me in my head. "Don't be that guy. Don't be that guy," I kept repeating to myself. It was a reminder to slow down a little on the drinking. Of course, the other part of my brain was saying "Be that guy! Chicks love a guy who is so drunk they piss themselves publicly."

Shortly after that, I remember Wiebe and I sitting on the sidewalk crying with laughter at God-knows-what. At some point in our escapades, we had been reunited with the two couples who came with us. They looked like they had a couple's night in New Orleans because they didn't look like they were having fun at all. We didn't care. New Orleans isn't really a street you want to take someone who you plan on marrying someday, in my opinion. The girls looked angry, and the guys looked at tits. Wiebe says to me, "Dude, I need to piss. I'm going inside this place. None of you leave me!" I remember sitting there for what seemed like forever, and Kristen finally says, "Davin, please go in there and check on Wiebe. Make sure he's not dead. He's been in there forever."

I walk inside this club, and it is jam packed, shoulder to shoulder. Apparently, this club didn't have any concerns about fire safety. I'm walking around looking over the sea of heads trying to identify Wiebe's haircut. There were so many people dancing. You actually had to dance your way through the club, it was so crowded. You dance on one girl, move on. Dance on one girl, move on. Dance on one guy. Apologize. "Sorry man, nice ass though." Finally, I'm dancing my way through the crowd, and I hear someone shouting, "Davin! Davin!" I turn around and Wiebe is staring at me with this huge smile on his face while this girl is grinding on his junk. He yells, "I tried to dance to the bathroom, and this happened!" I'm not kidding when I say it was an orgy of dancing. It was like the entire club was filled with single people just dry humping each other, which I gladly joined in with several nice young ladies. Wiebe and I bump and grinded our way to the bathroom. We walk into the bathroom and become dumbfounded. The mood instantly changed. We're staring at this... horse trough... over-flowing with brown urine. The entire floor was wet, and the smell was enough to make your eyes water. I don't think I'll ever forget that smell. It was so thick you could've poured it over pancakes. The trough was dripping urine like someone turned on a faucet of piss. Wiebe says, "Well fuck, we might as well pee on the floor then?" I agreed and we contributed to the problem by picking a corner and doing our business. That might sound a little messed up but you had to have seen this thing. If we pissed in it, it just would've gone on the floor anyway. Even though I know it was the wrong thing to do, trust me when I say it didn't make a lick of difference. If anything, our yellow urine added some color to the shit-brown urine in the trough. We finally walk back out into the club and in the exact same way we came in, we had to dance our way out.

The final thing I remember from that night is as we were walking back to our hotel, the three single guys and couples were talking about all the things we had experienced when we separated from each other. In the midst of this conversation, Matt interrupts and says, "Um, fellas. I think that lady is jerking off." We look over and there was this poor, homeless woman literally laying on the sidewalk, covered in a blanket. Now while the site of the homeless is always sad, she did not look sad at all. About waist high, her blanket was shaking vigorously. It looked like she was doing the down-town-Lester-Brown. Self-therapy, if you will. The sadness of seeing the homeless was overtaken by the hilarity of this lady flicking her bean and not giving a shit who saw.

After that moment, it was lights out for me. I woke up in our hotel room at 2:00 in the afternoon with the taste of vomit in my mouth, wearing my shirt but not wearing my pants. I have absolutely no recollection of how I got back to the car or back to the hotel room or why I wasn't wearing pants. My last memory was around 1:00/2:00 A.M. and I was told we returned to the hotel at 6:00 A.M. So, there's four hours of unaccounted fun lost forever. As of this writing, Michael, Wiebe, and I haven't spoken in years. We still occasionally keep up with each other on social media. We've all moved on, have our own lives. They have families now, but there was a time whenever we would call each other, talk about that night and how epic it truly was for a couple of teenagers from a small town to have the Bourbon Street experience. It's just one of those moments you could never duplicate with your very best friends, and I probably didn't even do it justice with the story I just wrote. It still holds a very special place in my heart, and I love telling the story to anyone who will listen.

I will probably never return there as Bourbon Street seems like a young man's place to party. My first and only experience is one I will cherish forever and one I don't want replaced. So, here's to you Bourbon Street, to the goth chick who ripped us off, to the frat guy who bought us the drinks, to the cop who didn't arrest us, to the clubs who didn't ID us, to the guy who pissed himself, and to the homeless lady who pleasured herself, cheers.

FOOTBALL ISN'T FOR ME

Football has never been kind to me my entire life. I have been physically, but mostly mentally, damaged over the years due to my feeble attempts at trying to play the sport. And all this abuse stemmed from a single moment during recess in eighth grade in Willow Springs, Missouri. A group of about thirty children who knew what they were doing, and then me, were playing a game of Hot Cement Skull Collision, also known as street football. I'm not sure of the rules of street football but from my experience, I think the rules were to go home with a new scab and nickname every day. So, there I was, Open Wound McButterfingers, near the touchdown line and this kid threw this Hail Mary pass. I remember looking at this watermelon-sized bullet gliding through the air and in the only cool football moment of my life, I jumped above the heads of every other kid and snatched the football. It was my very first touchdown ever. For a kid who collects coins and was very interested in chess, I was stoked! The kid who threw the ball even said to me afterwards, "That was a stud muffin catch there, Butterfingers." He still had to rub my nose in the dirt a little but I had a moment, and because of that moment, I thought I was ready for the big leagues.

I was so wrong.

After that day, my long-lost buddy, Timothy Miller, who was a big kid, convinced me we should try out for the football team. "With my size and your speed, dude, we'd be unstoppable." He was wrong. I was very stoppable which I found out very early in my practice sessions. I was basically a stop sign wearing a football helmet. On the first day of tryout, the Coach had all the players run this drill. If any of you athletes out there are reading this, you probably know the name of the drill I'm about to describe. I have since forgotten the name probably due to the amount of head injuries I sustained during it. Basically, one kid stands in the middle of a circle, running in place, surrounded by other players who I would describe as the size of my big brother. The other players would randomly attack you and try to tackle you to the ground. The goal of the exercise was to stay alert, be aware of your surroundings, dodge any players that tried to knock you down. The Coach sent me to do the drill first, I guess because he needed a good laugh that day.

So, there I was, HitHimHard McEasyPrey, in the middle of the circle, surrounded by six dudes ready to prove to their Coach they're ready for the Superbowl. The Coach would blow his whistle and the pain was soon to follow. One by one, one after the other, these guys just mowed over me. It wasn't so much as a football training session as it was legal public bullying. Ironically, the players were hitting me to the ground like they were spiking a football. "Get up," Coach would yell. I get up and get rammed from behind. "Get up, Davis!" I get up again and taken out from the side. I think those players on the outside must've thought I was actually the other team. "Get up," the Coach would yell again while all the now-sympathetic players were looking at me like, "Dude, stay down." You would think at some point there would be a mercy rule. Like the Coach would think, "This kid has been hit so much, I'm starting to think that's what he thinks he's supposed to be doing." But no, there was no mercy rule. There was no whistle blow to end my torture. Maybe only two minutes went by in reality, but by the end of my public humiliation, it felt like ten minutes me of being kicked in the balls. My everything hurt. The Coach finally blew his whistle and now it was my turn on the outside of the circle.

So, there I was, "Easily Bruised McGrassyStains", now on the outside ready to take my revenge on the teammates that had wronged me. It was even worse than being on the inside. When you're on the inside of that circle, you're the underdog. You're supposed to have the odds stacked against you. It's one versus six. Now, I'm on the six versus one side. The Coach blows his whistle and after the first two of my teammates tried to tackle this guy, they missed. He dodged them both perfectly. Like it was second nature to him. So now I'm thinking in my head, "What if I'm the guy to tackle him? I'll redeem myself in front of Coach!" So, I charge this refrigerator of a kid and he didn't even blink. He simply put up both is forearms and braced for impact as I charged him with the force of a thousand suns and ended up clotheslining myself to the ground. It was like throwing a dart at a tank. It's the only time I've had the air knocked out of me from both the front and the back. As I tried to catch my breath, I was still aware I needed to move before this kid beats me to death with another kid. I didn't walk out of the circle. I didn't crawl. I rolled. In football pads. Every time I rolled onto my shoulders the football pads would lift me off the ground slightly. I rolled out of the circle of pain into the land of defeat and more pain. This was the first drill on the first day of football. Clearly, I was the breakout star.

After that day I decided, right now, football isn't for me. I became paranoid after that day of practice. I can say it did help me become more aware of my surroundings because I was scared the Coach would pop out of a trash can as I'm walking home from school and headbutt me in the chest. "BAM! Lesson one, Davis, always be ready." Then he'd pee on me and leave.

Eventually, I moved to Pearl, Mississippi and I don't think I have to tell you, Mississippi is a football state. Every town in that state loves them some football. The football players at my high school were some of the most popular kids, at least to me, and I somehow wanted to make myself involved. I wanted to be cool like them. I wanted to walk around on non-game days in my football jersey in ninety-degree weather. So, what did I do? I joined the football team again.

As the water boy.

Not the cool Adam Sandler <u>Water Boy</u> who you later discover is a powerhouse of defense. Nope. The water boy who was so weak and skinny, he couldn't even carry the barrel-sized Gatorade cooler from the locker room to the benches. I was only the water boy for two games during my ninth-grade year. The very first game was an away game and I had to carry the barrels of water from the bus to the locker room, and from the locker room to the football field. It was already second quarter by the time I made it out there. The second time I was the water boy was during a home game and after having to carry, nay, drag this thing in front of cheerleaders and my hometown so pathetically, I decided once again, football isn't for me. Hell, collecting water isn't for me either apparently. I didn't even tell the Coach or the players. I just stopped showing up and nobody ever said anything to me about it, so I think it was an amicable decision that I was off the team.

I still did want to play football though for one reason and one reason only. Not for the glory, not for the cheerleader's praise, not for the roar of the crowd as you score a touchdown. You gaze into the crowd and see your dad give you a teary-eyed "I'm proud of you" look. Those things were great, sure, but I wanted something more.

All I wanted to do was talk at our pep rallies.

You see at my high school, Pearl High School (Go Pirates!), we would hold our pep-rallies inside our school gymnasium for the Pearl Pirates football team. If you ever played in a gym, then you know the acoustics are horrible. Every little thing echoes. They were still entertaining though. The cheerleaders would dance and do amazing gymnastics. The drumline would do these very cool sounding percussion performances. The goth kids would sit in the stands and write poems about back acne. Whatever. At the end of most of the pep rallies though, there would be a microphone setup connected to speakers. The school would allow two or three players to get on the mic and basically trash talk the opposing team while getting the crowd hyped for the game. The problem was the horrible acoustics, so you never understood a single word the players would say. You could literally get in front of the mic and yell, "Pickles are just hydrated cucumbers" and the crowd would go ape shit. They'd cheer and scream like they just heard a Hulk Hogan promo. "Yeah! Woooo, go Pirates!"

All I wanted to do was talk into that microphone and try to see what I could get away with saying. I would've volunteered every week. Say things like, "I haven't talked to my Dad in eight years! We have a really strained relationship!" Then the DJ at the pep rally would play that song, "Let's Get Ready To Rumbleeeeeeee" as cheerleaders did flips in front of my stupid crying face. Or better yet, I wanted a player on the team who had zero confidence.

"Yeah, it's not looking good. Our quarterback is injured. We haven't beaten these guys in 16 years. I got to be honest, things are looking very bleak."

Then the DJ pipes in, "EVERYBODY DANCE NOW!"

I was one of those kids who really enjoyed high school and have so many great memories from there, but again, football isn't for me.

PUBLICLY HUMILIATED ON VALENTINE'S DAY

I love to write. If you've been my friend for a while, you know this. It's almost therapeutic for me. So, with Max, my cat, recently passing away (more on him later), I decided instead of being publicly depressed, I would try to think of something funny to talk on my page about Valentine's Day.

This happened to me in high school, and I'm not going to name the names of the girls involved because I'm still friends with them both on social media and it's still embarrassing. You probably know who you are once you read this. Not mad about it, you were just part of one of my most embarrassing high school moments.

So, it's Valentine's Day, 9th grade. I don't know if your school did this, but for Valentine's Day at every year, you could buy three different types of roses. Red, which basically meant I love you. Yellow, which meant I like you or I have a crush on you. Or white, which meant basically I like our friendship and I'm too much of a coward to tell you how I really feel. So, there was this girl I had a *huge* crush on, and she had a name very similar to this other girl in our high school. There was only a two-letter difference in the name. So, on Valentine's Day, I was going to confess my love for this girl by buying her five red roses. To this day I can't remember why I chose five. I guess I was like, "I gave you five roses. Do you want to touch it now?" The students who worked in the office would then deliver them throughout the day.

Well, there was a mix-up.

I was in class with the *other* girl when the door opens, and this delivery girl walks up to this other girl and hands her my roses with a "From Davin" label on them. The other girl first goes "Awwww!" cause she thought they were from her boyfriend (who was a senior, by the way). Yes, the office unintentionally sent flowers with my name on it to the wrong girl who had a boyfriend. She reads the label with my name on it, turns around to me and goes, "Ummmm, no thank you" and tells her friend to pass me back my flowers, IN FRONT OF THE CLASS! I was so confused for a second. I thought someone sent her flowers, she didn't want them, turned to me and was thinking, "Davin's ugly, here, you can have them." Then I realized what had happened. The office messed up and gave the wrong girl my flowers. Now I couldn't just leave class and march to the office as an unsatisfied customer. "Hey! You gave my flowers to the wrong woman. I want my money back, Principal Asshole." So, once I realize what happened, I told her "Oh, no, these weren't supposed to go to you" to which she instantly replied, "Good!" And it was a hard "good," she really emphasized the GUUH sound in "Good!" So now it looks like I was in love with her and gave her flowers. I repulsed her so she shot me down in front of God and everybody, and then I tried to save it by being like, "Oh, those weren't supposed to go to you," so now I look like a complete and total tool.

I had a class with the right girl two classes later. Already embarrassed as hell being turned down by a girl I wasn't even trying to ask out, I was debating about giving her (the right girl) the flowers. I walk into class and she's sitting at her desk already. I sit down in the desk beside her, and my heart sank. In front of her, she has three red roses, three white roses, a yellow rose. She might as well as had a giant teddy bear with a heart on it that said, "Everyone wants to fuck me." Apparently, I'm not the only dude, or female, who thought this chick was beautiful. We were only good friends in high school, so when she sees the flowers I'm holding, she says "Awww, who sent you those?" And I, dear reader, completely chickened out. I just said, "I'm not sure, it didn't come with a card."

The next morning in the commons area, the other girl's boyfriend (who, thank goodness, was a nice guy) walks up to me and goes, "Hey man, did you give [his girlfriend] flowers yesterday?" I said "Yeah, but not on purpose, they were supposed to go to [the girl I had a crush on.]" I tell him the whole story, he starts cracking up and, with this being icing on the cake, he goes "You dodged a bullet dude. I think she likes girls."

So, if I had given her the flowers, not only would I have given the wrong girl flowers and got shot down, but I would've also given a lesbian flowers and got shot down. A double whammy. Turns out, I found out years later on social media she wasn't a lesbian.

High school was complicated.

SHOULD'VE DRAWN SOME FRUIT

For legal reasons, I'm going to say that the story you're about to read is entirely fictional. We all on the same page on this one? This story is not real.

When I was in 9th grade, and 10th grade, and 11th grade, I had the worst teacher I've ever had. I moved a lot when I was a kid. I've lived all over the United States: Virginia, Mississippi, Louisiana, Missouri, South Carolina, and several others and out of everywhere I lived, this teacher was a demon from the sixth circle of hell. He was one of two Pearl High School's art teachers in Pearl, Mississippi. Now for legal reasons I can't say his name because I'm about to talk mad shit on this guy, so let's just call him by a fake name, Mr. Cox.

I do have friends on social media that can confirm he was the worst teacher in the history of teachers. That might be too crude. He was the worst teacher of students who loved art. And he was *the* art teacher at Pearl High School (Go Pirates! I sucked at football!). I had one paddling from the principals in my entire school life and it was because of Mr. Cox. And I'm going to tell you that story.

Now Mr. Cox was a balding, 40-something year old guy with a pornstache who talked with a lisp and told the worst dad jokes. That's actually insulting to Dads. He told terrible jokes ALL. THE. TIME. If he was a stand-up comedian, he would've gotten heckled every class period. And because of his lisp, everyone was absolutely 100% sure he was a closeted gay man. "Not that there's anything wrong with that," to quote Jerry Seinfeld. But, come on bro, you got a pornstache, you have a lisp, you teach art. You're gay, bruh. It's okay, don't be ashamed, let that fag flag fly high and proud. No judgement here. Students would write over his name plate that was outside of his class all the time, "Mr. Cox". Children are mean. Honestly, there were tons of gay students at that school, and nobody really gave a damn. It's just this guy was such a douchebag that they used being gay as an insult to him, even though most of us at that school had gay friends.

It's like, "Yeah, Paul's cool. He's gay but he's cool dude. But Mr. Cox is a butt pirate. Anyway, you guys want to go lick ice cream cones together while staring into each other's eyes?"

To give one example of how much of a douche canoe this dude was, one time in the 11th grade, we had a kid in our class named Jeremiah. And on the first day of class, he roll-called Jeremiah, and Jeremiah said "here." And Mr. Cox said "Jeremiah, are you a bullfrog?" and he starts laughing. Hysterically. Shoulders bobbing up and down. Giggling hard. And no one else in the class got the joke from his 70's song reference. And he says, almost angrily, "How come no one's laughing?!" which just made it worse. Cringe-worthy.

So, if you don't know, I love art. I love drawing, painting, making comic book strips, logos, t-shirts. I've always enjoyed art since I was a small child. And Mr. Cox, he wasn't exactly revolutionary in his art style. For months and months of school, me, and several other hundred PHS students, had to paint bowls of fruit. The lamest thing ever to paint and we had to do it all the time. Over and over and over again. When you came to class and saw a bowl of fruit set up, you'd be like "NOOOOOO! Not again." It was torture for us art lovers.

So, one day in Mr. Cox's class, we had a "draw whatever you want" day. Probably the lazy day for art teachers. And at the time I was a huge *Johnny The Homicidal Maniac* comic book fan. He was drawn by the same guy who did the more famous *Invader Zim* show. Jhonen Vasquez was the artist. Now Johnny The Homicidal Maniac is not pop culture but google it. The comic is very violent, dark, and also super hilarious, so I wanted to do an ink and pen comic drawing tribute of JTHM. And I start drawing it and it's turning out so sick, if I do say so myself.

And Mr. Cox walks by my desk, he stops, he back peddles, and he quizzically looks at my drawing and goes "What is that?" And I explain to him he's a comic book character I just discovered that I'm in love with. And Mr. Cox snatches, SNATCHES, the pen from my hand and goes, "Yeah but he needs a background though" and starts inking these lame ass trees into my picture's background. His art style is in no way even comes close to matching my art style (or should I say Jhonen's) and he, as far as I'm concerned, just ruined my drawing. Ruins it. It looks like trash now in my eyes.

I got so pissed. Even if you're not an artist, imagine if you painted your house in the colors you wanted to paint it. And then someone who sold you the paint at Wal-Mart comes over to your house and starts painting the walls of your house diarrhea green. And you're like, "I don't want my child's room to be diarrhea green" and he goes, "You're welcome. I made it better." That's what it felt like. What kind of art teacher just draws over the artistic creativity of their students? Why am I even drawing in the first place then? That's bullshit. If you want to show me how to draw a background, draw it on your own piece of paper or the giant chalk board surrounding the class you butt pirate. You're raping the artistic creativity of students you're teaching art to with your fruity pen. Just so you know, if you're an art teacher and you do that, you're an asshole. You are. I hate to be the one to break it to you, but you are. Stop teaching art and kill yourself.

Can you tell I was angry?

Well on the particular day he drew on my drawing, he called half the class into his office about a half an hour into the class to explain his next, super creative, fruit painting project. "Instead of grapes this week, you'll be painting long, hard, throbbing bananas" or whatever he said. So, half the class leaves to go to his office, and I'm still white-hot mad. They go into this side room, his office, for him to discuss his next stupid project and there's a window where you can see into his office. I get up from my desk and walk to window and I just let it rip. I violently flip him the bird. I gave him the universe's most powerful middle finger. Dear reader, it was so good. It opened a black hole it was so good. I saw students in the room laughing and I quickly ran back to my seat before he saw me. The class comes back into the room and Mr. Cox walks right up to me and goes, "Davin, come to my office." Oh shit, someone tattled on me. (I know who it was but I'm over it. It's been 15 years. I'm fine now, Amanda.)

He goes, "When I was talking to the students, one of them said you raised your middle finger to me." Raise your middle finger? Who says that? So, I try to pull the whole, "Whaaaaaa? Nah, I didn't do that." Then he changed his story. "Well, several students said you did." Okay now SEVERAL students saw it? I said, "No sir, no I didn't." And he goes "Okay yeah you did for sure," and he starts writing me a detention slip aggressively. He hands it to me and goes, "Go to the principal's office, now!"

I go and I walk to the front desk of the office and this student goes, "How can I help you?" And I don't say anything, I just hand her the slip of paper. She looks at it, smiles, and goes, "Right this way," with an almost creepy smile like she's the gimp in Pulp Fiction and happy someone else is about to be punished. I go into the office and one of the principals mispronounces my name and says, "Daven, why are you here?" And I was honest.

I said, "I was drawing a picture in art class, and Mr. Cox ruined it and I got mad and flipped him off." And the principal, Mr. Craven, goes "Was it worth it?" And I said, "I'm not sure yet." He tells me, "Well let's find out," and he tells me to bend over and put my hands against the wall. He grabs a wooden paddle and goes, "Okay, here we go. 1, 2, 3..." and gives me 5 really hard whacks. Swack! Swack! Swack! Swack! Swack!

It, really, really hurt. Tears were forming in my eyes. Manly tears though, but tears none the less. The principal goes, "Okay, you're done. Go back to class." And I left his office. And I B-lined it back to class, fighting tears or at least trying to. Life hack kids: Don't ever cry at school after getting paddled. I was so upset that I felt I was unjustly punished for a crime that was so worthy to commit. I get back to Mr. Cox's class and Mr. Cox greets me at the door. And he whispers like a molesty, Catholic priest right next to my ear...

"So did you learn anything?"

I just couldn't help myself. I said, "I learned you shouldn't draw backgrounds on other people's art." And instantly, he wrote me a second detention slip right then and there for Saturday detention. What did he expect me to say? Seriously. "Thank you so much for drawing on my portrait and then sending me to the office to get punished. I have learned a valuable lesson and hope I can continue to learn more from you." No. Fuck you dude. I guess I could've handled the situation a little better. It was just a drawing. I could always draw another picture. Maybe I shouldn't have flipped him off behind his back, and instead, do it to his face. Maybe not at all. But at the time, I didn't care. My emotions told me what to do and I followed suit. Felt good and right at the time.

Anyway, I had to come in on the next Saturday for detention.

I go in for Saturday detention and the guy running it was our black P.E. coach whose name I forget. Like I said, this was my only detention ever and the only interaction I've ever had with this guy. And, ironically, he was also an artist. He painted nothing but Black Jesus paintings. I'm not kidding. There were pictures of Black Jesusesesses everywhere in the room. The entire detention room was surrounded by Black Jesus paintings like some sort of cult. I know everyone reading this who I went to high school with know what I'm talking about.

He walks by my desk at one point, and, still fanboying, I'm drawing JTHM, and he goes, "What's that?" I explain who JTHM is and how he's responsible for Mr. Cox giving me Saturday detention. And in a moment of pure awesomeness this Saturday morning P.E. coach, who is also an artist says...

"Should've drawn some fruit." And smiled.

JAIL FOOD AND LUBE

I'm not proud of it. What I'm about to tell you is not my shiniest of moments in life, but it did happen. Remember, when this happened, I was a much younger, stupider man back then. This happened 2 weeks ago. I'm going to tell you about the time I went to jail.

When I first got to the magical enchanted land of Jail World, they put me in a drunk tank, if that gives you any clue as to why I was there. The drunk tank is the urine crusted holding cell they put you in when you first arrive to sober up, or remove the pills from your butt, even though I wasn't drunk by the time I arrived, nor high. I was getting high off the fumes of the urine though. It was butter thick. After about what felt like an hour, two guards came to the door and go "Daven Davis (are you seeing a pattern in my life with my name?), you need to strip and put this on." They were holding an orange jump suit. First time in my life two men watched me strip naked and no one made it rain. That's just bullying. You make me strip naked and don't even tip to see all this cash and prizes I got going on underneath. They did make me spread my butt cheeks and cough in case I actually was hiding pills or a weapon in my bum.

I've often wondered about people hiding things up in their ass. You would think at some point in your life, when you're shoving a pill bottle of heroin up your ass, you might ask yourself, "Who am I? Should I change the direction of my life? Nah. Now let's get back to being a heroin mule." I accidentally fell on a hot tub water pressure pipe when I was 12 and I can absolutely confirm I never want anything to ever enter that crevasse again. It never called me back. But I digress.

After I got the jump suit on, they handcuffed me and walked me to a cell. Not going to lie, it actually kind of felt badass. I was already coming up with my story in my head I was going to tell people when they asked.

"What are you in for?"

"I stabbed the president."

They took me to this hexagonal room where other inmates are sleeping. There was no room to sit down. I mean, none. Everybody had already found their spot on the floor and there was this tiny two inch by two inch opening between feet I managed to sit down in. The guard apologized to me and said the reason these rooms were so cramped is because they were in the middle of transporting prisoners. I don't mean people in for a DUI like myself. I mean people in prison for things like murder, assault, jaywalking. I don't know if he meant to scare the shit out of me by explaining I could be sharing the room with murderers, but he did.

Inside the cell with me was this old, gray-stubbled white guy who kept bringing up the fact that he was going to sue the cops for arresting him. When I said, "Can I ask what you did," he said, "I threw a remote at my wife and she called the cops on me!" Well, sounds like an open and shut case bro. Good luck on your millions you'll win with the lawyer who won't take your case.

Also inside the cell was this clearly scared young kid. I asked him why he was there, and he said he was in jail for "stealing lube from Wal-Mart." Stealing lubricate. From Wal-Mart. If that's not the lamest reason to be inside a jail cell. "You don't know me man! I've done things! Lots of things, smothered with lube. My penis slides in easily anywhere!" Actually, now that I think about it, that could be a little scary. At one point he announced out loud to the room, "I'm just looking around here to see what I can use as a weapon." Sorry little guy. Looks like the only weapon is this sleeping mat that smells like feet.

The creepiest dude in there was this old black guy with a long gray beard and bright yellow eyes. I mean the whites in his eyes were bright yellow. I've never seen anyone in real life with such a failed liver. He almost looked demonic. And this dude had the longest, brownest, greenest toenail I have ever seen. It was on his big toe and I'm not exaggerating when I say this thing was three inches long. I'm pretty sure the reason why he was in jail was he killed someone in an alcoholic rage and his toenail was the murder weapon. It was cracked, growing crooked and just gross. Believe it or not, that wasn't the grossest thing about this gentleman. At one point, and I have no idea why he was doing this, he started hocking loogies onto the crotch of his pants and then smearing the loogies into the pants with his hand. Just as I typed that sentence, my spine shivered. It looked more gross than it sounds. Imagine me: young, first time in jail and my cell mate is an old black man with demon eyes, spitting loogies into this crotch with the world's crustiest toenail pointing at you sideways

Eventually, the door to the cell opens, and a jail guard and a big Native American dude in an orange jump suit with both his feet and arms handcuffed are standing there. The guard says, "Who's Daven Davis?" I reply, "I am." He goes "We're sending you to Max." Now, when he said, "sending you to Max" I thought Max was some big bubba trucker dude who gets first dibs with the new fish, if you smell what the Rock is cooking. I paused, cause like I said, I thought the guard was being so casual about my future rape. I go "...Who's Max?" The cop and the prisoner next to him both start laughing. The guard goes, "No, maximum security." I think that might've been the only time in human history someone heard the phrase, "We're taking you to maximum security" and they were relieved. That relief only lasted a few seconds when I realized they're sending me to maximum security... maximum security... maximum security... You know, the rape-y part of jail.

As the guard already explained, these rooms were full because they were transferring prisoners from another prison, and they were all being held here until they moved on to the next prison. I thought about stealing black dudes' crusty toenail and using it as a weapon in case things got hairy.

They handcuffed me and walked me to an elevator. When we got inside the elevator, it didn't have the traditional row of buttons, just one button. I don't know if we went upstairs or downstairs but when we got to the destination, to say it was off-putting would be an understatement. The doors open, and there it was: Maximum Security. Maximum security was very dark and very cramped. It looked like the set of a movie, just something you don't see in your everyday life. I don't know how to explain the vibe walking through that place. It was almost other worldly. You're walking through and all these dudes are just staring you down, sizing you up. None of the stares look welcoming. The looks were like a hungry wolf just noticed a baby dear.

We get to my cell and there are two prisoners already in the cell asleep. The big Native American dude and I are about to join them. The guard wakes them up from their sleep by banging on their cell with his club. He explains to them we are their new cell mates. The first dude sits up, jumps out of his bed and the first two things I notice is: This is a muscular dude, and he has the word "Stephens" tattooed across his giant shoulders on his back. He doesn't look at us. He just starts angrily tossing books and other things off an unused bed. The second dude stands up to join and he's towering. Professional basketball player height. His name, Too Tall. He had "2Tall" tattooed on his neck. I started to wonder if you must get your name tattooed on you when you're in jail, so you don't forget who you are. "I've done thirty years! I don't even know who I am anymore!" 2tall was a lifer he later explained to me. In prison for the rest of his life. So, he didn't have anything to lose which I was very excited about.

They clear off the beds. The Native American dude and me walk in there. I've seen enough prison movies and documentaries to know you have to be very careful where you step, where you put things. Prisoners can get easily offended if you touch something that doesn't belong to you or walk in a territory you're not welcomed. So, I'm just standing there, not moving an inch, holding my blanket, not wanting to be shanked by anyone's toenail. Stephens just kind of looks at us sideways, like a confused dog, and goes "Well, get your asses up there. We didn't clear this off for nothing." I got top bunk. I jump on the bed and first thing I noticed was the toilet.

The toilet was right in the middle of the room, just off to the side of being in the middle of the beds. Meaning if you're dropping a deuce, the whole world can watch. Worst of all, there was very little toilet paper left, and I wasn't sure if there was a suck-a-dick fee to get it. "Looks like I'll be wiping my ass with my pants leg, so I don't get jumped for using the last of the toiletries."

Stephens and 2tall go right back to sleep like nothing happened, and I just laid on the bed questioning my life choices and wondering how I could turn a blanket into a knife. I soon fell asleep just hoping by the time I woke up it would be time for me to get out on Monday.

You have no sense of time when you're behind bars. Like I said, I've seen movies and documentaries and I've heard prisoners say that and its absolutely true. You don't know if it's 2:00 in the afternoon or 3:00 in the morning. There are no clocks. No sunshine. Nothing. Shortly thereafter, they brought us food. Let me describe what they call "food."

First of all, it was served on a tray that still had clearly old food dried on it. Like they just ran it under the faucet and that was it. No soap, no scrubbing. Just dirty prison water and called it good. The entrée was "ham," which to me looked like the skin of a sun burned ass cheek. The ham looked like it had psoriasis. Next to that was what I thought was grits. Turned out to be watered down mashed potatoes with a special ice chunk filling in the middle. Then, to keep healthy, a dried-out orange slice like in junior high, and a tiny carton of milk. Honestly, the black guy's toenail looked more appetizing. I took one bite of the ass ham and after discovering the ice chunk in the potatoes, I decided I wasn't hungry.

When Stephens and 2tall woke up, we got to talking and Stephens asked me who I knew in my hometown. I just started naming names and when I said "Tracy," he was like "Ooooh yeah, Tracy a girl?" I go "Yeah." He goes "Mmmmmm what she look like though?" I go "...she's pretty." He goes "Mmmmmmmm yeeeeeah." I think he was getting a raging semi just by saying a girl's name. Probably been a while since he seen a woman.

I quickly changed topics before that semi turned into a full-blown seven inch and I started asking questions about them. I found out then that the reason Stephens and 2Tall are cell mates is because they fought each other earlier in the week. That's right, these two got into a fight, tried to kill each other, and the guards decided they should be roommates like some sort of fucked up sitcom, and they threw me in there with them. I didn't ask why they fought. I just moved right away from that question. "Yeah, we're in here for fighting each other." "Oh really, that's cool. Do you guys like beef jerky?"

I did my hard time of two days in the slammer. The inside changes a man, ya know. Eventually, Monday came along, and it was time for me to leave. I'm not going to lie, being in a maximum-security jail was one of the scariest days of my life. I get sad when I see a dead squirrel on the side of the road, and I'm trapped in a place with people who stabbed their own family. However, Stephens and 2Tall were good dudes who just seemed to have made some bad decisions in life. I'm not going to pretend I know them, but they were nice to me, Thank Goodness. And I didn't have to perform felatio on anyone or have my butt intruded so all in all I would give it three stars on Yelp. The food sucked. The sleeping mats smelled like dead foot. I had to shit in front of strangers. But I made friends with violent criminals. And, I can always say I survived maximum security and I wouldn't be lying. I didn't get one of those cool teardrop tattoos on my face which I think you get after you shank a punk bitch. Every now and then when I pass by the jail, 2tall and Stephens cross my mind. Don't let them keep you down homies. They can jail your body but not your mind. Word life.

MAX STEALS THE TOILET PAPER

I'm going to tell you a story. A true story, that happens to me every single day of my life. It happens to everyone who comes over to my house and uses my bathroom. Each story has a different variation, but the same core thing happens in each story.

My cat, Maximus, has figured out how to open the bathroom door.

Besides him figuring out he can climb curtains, or him finding out that food comes out of a trash can if it's knocked over (and that it scares the hell out of me in the middle of the night) him entering the bathroom is the worst new skill he has acquired. My other cat, Sheldon, learned months ago that fresh running water comes out of the bathroom sink. He just needs someone to turn it on for him. Yaaaay. Both of my shedding, annoying, constant-need-of-attention cats have learned tricks during your special private time.

Now opening that particular bathroom door isn't hard, because if you don't shut it just the right way, all it takes is a little force and just like that, the door is now open. Max has figured this out. So, every time me or anyone else uses the bathroom, this is what will happen.

If you have to go #1, you will start walking to the bathroom. If Sheldon sees you in time, he will dart in front of you from any direction like a ninja cat and try to trip you, hoping you fall and hit your head on the bookshelf, causing you to have a stroke while bleeding to death on the floor. Or at least that's the scenario I see in my head every time he does that. I have stepped on him accidentally and he has made me fall to the ground. One time he tripped me, and I grabbed a broom for leverage. Obviously, the broom didn't hold up and it came down with me and side of the bristles smacked my forehead. Asshole. Anyways, he will run into the bathroom. He will look at you with these cute little asshole eyes. You'll turn the water on for him, and this part is important, if you turn the water on for too long, Sheldon will drink too much, and vomit. Trust me, it has happened enough times to where I needed to figure out why he was doing it so much.

You shut the door and you start urinating. At this point, you will hear a "dragging" sound like something out of a horror movie. You will turn around you will see this gray-and-white claw coming in from underneath the door, latching onto the ground and pushing the door open. This is, of course, Maximus coming in to let you know he has to meow 42 times and attacks Sheldon tail when Sheldon is drinking on the sink. While you are peeing, Max will sit-up on the toilet, and get within CENTIMETERS OF YOUR PEE STREAM, and stare off into the toilet like it's the Fountain of Youth. You can't fight him with your feet either, we all know how out-of-control peeing can get. One time, he saw his reflection in the toilet and swatted at it. Then freaked out and ran out the bathroom, all this happening in between my legs. You then stop, cut the water off for Sheldon, shut the lid, flush the toilet and now you have two cats walking around your feet as you zip up, making sure not to step on or trip over them. However, in Cat Land, you must walk extra slowly and in zigzags. It's a rule, I'm sure of it. If you're lucky, Max will decide to pick a fight with Sheldon as you walk.

Now, that is what happens when you go #1. When you do the other thing (poop, heh), you will walk to the bathroom. Sheldon will do his cat jujitsu and dart out of some unseen corner trying to beat you to the bathroom to make sure you don't drink his sink water. If you don't trip and die, you will cut the water on for Sheldon and you sit down. Now, you never noticed this when you were peeing, but your back was turned to Sheldon. Now, when you sit down, you're facing, not him, but his cat butthole, that is just sitting there, tail up, staring back at you like the Egyptian eye. You'll think "Okay, today's off to a good start already." Then, as you're sitting there on your phone, trying to ignore cat butt, you'll hear the meowing and the scratches. You'll see Maximus' little gray and white paw come under the door, push the door open, and now as your stink and business is exposed to the world, he will come in to let you know that he has just meowed and he's going to do it again 41 more times. And from this point on, who knows what wacky adventure he's about to take you on.

One time he opened the door, saw the toilet paper sitting on the ground, pounced on it, and rolled it out of the bathroom down the hall. I was left stranded with the door wide open yelling a cat to bring me back the toilet paper. Spoiler: he didn't. One time, he jumped on the top shelf that sits behind the toilet and knocked over one of those smell-good spray cans, hitting me in the back of the head. One time he went to jump on the sink,

I guess to show me his cat butthole, but he didn't know there was a comb up there. He hits the comb making him slip, comb falls to the floor at the same time he falls on my legs. The comb scares the shit out of him, and he leaves me three Wolverine claw marks on my foot as he used it to get some running leverage.

He watches house guests pee and poop. No one has privacy in this house. He will try to jump and lay in your lap while you're sitting on the toilet. He will jump into the bathtub and just knock shit over for the f--- of it. Sheldon, not that disrespectful once he's in there. He ignores you; he patiently waits for you to finish while sipping on his cool nourishing faucet water. Not Max! Nooooo. Max will bite your toes, making you flinch too hard and jam your toes on the bottom of the cabinet.

The lock doesn't work and after a year, all this has become annoying. So now, I don't let the cats into the bathroom with me anymore. I actually have to race them in there. There is an electronic scale in my bathroom. I have figured out that I can jam it under the door like a last-ditch attempt to keep a murderer out, and because of its tread, Max can't push it open. Yet, he tries every time. I never thought I would have to be jamming electrical equipment under a door just so I could pee.

One time, I was awoken by having Maximus jump, from the floor to my bed, and land on my "no-jump-zone". I mean, bullseye. Right on the dick head and balls simultaneously. Snipers couldn't have hit it any better. I don't understand. I rescued you from a shelter. I gave you a home. I feed you. I change your litter box once every couple of months. I adopted you a friend too. And yet, you're always trying to kill me.

Now I feel bad because when Max did that, I yelled at him and he took off running, scared. I know he was just jumping on the bed to cuddle, but for a cat, a creature that has pinpoint accuracy when leaping, landed right on my sack of pain. Now I'm the bad guy because I'm sore. That's like some woman vagina voodoo magic. Fellas know what I'm talking about. Like when your girl is in the wrong, they hurt your feelings, you yell back, and now you feel bad cause they act all innocent like "what, I just wanted to love you." That's textbook woman-arguing psychology. Not trying to compare women to cats but in my defense, both have tried to kill me.

Sheldon, my other cat, is a very soft, loving cat. He's old, just wants to be left alone unless you're laying down, then he wants to lay with you. He loves it when you scratch his face. He's a Vietnam War survivor whose wife died of cholera. That's the background story I gave him. Just a sweet gentle cat on the other side of 50 years old.

Lord Maximus III on the other hand, is just, straight, butthole. I think he thinks like "I'm going to climb every curtain in the house with my razor-sharp claws. I will break all the blinds. I will try to escape every chance I get, and have you worried the whole time, even though I'm just hiding in the bushes. I will eat your food, spill your drinks, knock over your trash cans, and of course, hurt you in every way I can think of! Heh, hehehe, heheheh, hahahaha, HAHAHAhaha, HAHAHAHAHA, MOUHAHAHAHAH meow."

I keep hoping it's going to pay off adopting him. Like if my home is ever invaded, he's going to turn into Ninja Cat and just shred the invaders into noodles. But most likely he'll just pee on me as I'm being tied up and beaten, and then meow that his food bowl is empty as I lay in a blood puddle.

They were good cats. Despite all they did in my house, they brought a lot of joy and laughs into it as well. Sadly, they both passed in 2016 and 2017. I miss those guys.

Toenail People

There's something about me that gives people the impression that's it's okay to talk to me shortly after I wake up and when I find out what it is, I'm going to destroy it. People keep saying horrible things to me in the morning. Horrible things. Things like "Good morning" and "How are you?" What kind of asshole does that? I haven't had coffee yet and you're trying to have a polite conversation? No thank you to that.

I'm not a morning person. Never have been. Yet, people will see me in the morning and must think "He looks tired. Look at those bags under his eyes. I better have a conversation with him and give him 9 paragraphs of information to process. He'll appreciate that." I used to inadvertently hurt my mom's feelings when I was a teenager because she would ask me questions, multiple questions, right after I woke up. They would be normal questions too like "What are you doing today?" But that's not what I would hear. What I would hear is "How do I triangulate the hypotenuse of an acute right angle for which the answer = x?"

Morning people just don't get it. They'll tell you things like "Wanna wake up and go jogging up a hill? Maybe afterwards we'll go paint a barn." And you'll look at them in confusion like,"...Is there cocaine involved? Is the barn full of cocaine and Redbull?"

Anyone who knows me knows that I can easily and guilt-free sleep until 3:00 in the afternoon. And they'll say things like "You wasted your whole day. You didn't do anything." And I'll say back, "You wasted YOUR day by doing things. I slept until I was extremely well rested. Good luck with your nap that'll never happen, ya moron."

The worst is when someone tells you to wake up. "Wake up, Davin!" Telling someone who isn't a morning person to wake up, that's like telling an angry woman to calm down. Ever done that? Ever told an angry and upset woman to calm down? Try it some time. See how it works out for you. She'll appreciate the new and exciting information you have just provided for her to deal with her emotions. Or stab you. It's 50/50.

I had a co-worker named Nona who I love. Know why? Cause I see her every morning and she never says shit to me. Nothing. And I respect that.

Only thing she ever says is "Davin, here are your cookies." And I'm just like "Not only did you not ask anything of me, but you baked me sweet, delicious cookies. You are an angel."

Non-morning people and Talky McTalkersons are the worst. Mortal enemies. Because Talky McTalkersons will start talking to you for no reason about bullshit you don't care about. You didn't make eye contact. You didn't clear your throat. You did nothing to give off the persona that you want to make sentences with your word hole. Yet they'll just be like "The other day, Chapter 1, when I was four, stuff with things happened to blah blah who gives a shit right."

I want to be like "What did I do to inspire you to talk to me? Was it me answering your question with a grunt or was it me wiping the sleep crusties out of my eye?"

This scenario happens to me all the time. Almost every time I get off work, especially after a long day, I just want to go to the bar, have a beer and chill out. I spend hours of my day putting on a fake face, making sure customers and employees are happy, after dealing with mountains of bullshit I can't discuss on social media, walking on my feet for hours while hearing problems from the people I work with. And when I get off, I want to sit down, drink a nice cold beer and turn my brain off, and just chillllll...

And every. single. time., somebody at whatever bar I go to will interject my path, stop me, and tell me about their sad life problems I don't give a shit about. I'm sorry. I'm tired of being nice about it. This must stop. There are two pandemics going on in this world right now. One is Covid-19. The other is people who don't know their stories suck and they should shut the fuck up.

Maybe I would give a crap about your depressing life on my day off. But not today though. I just worked a twelve-hour shift. I don't care. Doesn't matter if I do care though because they wouldn't care either way. They just want to download their miseries into my brain as I keep looking over at the bar, screaming with my eyes for someone to save me. That's why I quit going out so much. I used to love going out. I used to love meeting strangers and listening to their stories. Now, go die.

Someone will be like, "Davin! Come here! Guess what? So, I guess you heard Carla has hemmotarded ingrown toenail syndrome?" And I'm just like, "I don't know who that is, or what the fuck that is, but... thoughts and prayers?" I don't understand the thought process behind that.

"Hey, you know this person you never hang out with, well I just thought you'd like to know their life is sad and depressing."

"Oh cool! Thanks! Now I can sleep better knowing about their toenail situation."

To be honest, ninety percent of the time, they're half drunk, half just want an ear to bitch too. And I understand that. I know I can have word vomit sometimes when I'm drunk. But eventually though, I pass out. These people have Duracell batteries plugged into their back. It doesn't matter what advice you try to give them either. They're not really looking for advice. They just want to talk over you, through you, around you, just to talk. And in their drunk head, they think they're giving the I Have a Dream speech, but most of the time they're just kind of admitting to crimes they probably shouldn't be telling anyone. Especially to me. I'll put it in a book. Let me give you a slightly exaggerated example below. This is typically how a conversation happens to me at a bar. Notice how I said, "how a conversation happens to me", like someone committed a hate crime against me.

Some Random Asshole: Oh, hey man! What's up?! Davin, right?

Me: Hey, sup?

Some Random Asshole: What have ya been up to?
Me: Oh, you know. Living the dream. Working all the time.

Some Random Asshole: Oh brother, tell me about it. I feel like that's all I do, work and eat. I could barely eat today though.

Me: Ok.

Some Random Asshole: Too much on my mind. I'm in town cause this girl I hooked up with 11 months ago is pregnant and I'm possibly the father.

Me: Mmhmm.

Some Random Asshole: I want to be a good father too unlike my piece of shit brother who's in jail. Drug trafficking and attempted murder.

Me: Damn, that's crazy.

Some Random Asshole: He ain't ever getting out, not that I really care though.

Me: Yeah?

Some Random Asshole: Now my sister is a real piece of work lemme tell ya.

Me: Please don't.

Some Random Asshole: Hooks up with guy after guy after guy, who the hell knows who her baby daddy is. Or should I say baby daddies?

Me: You're not even hearing me, are you?

Some Random Asshole: Just one kid after the other after the other. Hell, you know she's milking the government for everything.

Me: Sometimes when I get bored, I rip out pubes.

Some Random Asshole: I wasn't raised like that. I work for my money. I work for every damn thing I've ever owned; you feel me?

Me: I shaved your grandmother's ass with my teeth last night.

Some Random Asshole: Hell, my house, my truck, all that's paid for. Hell, I'd give anyone the shirt off my back. I ain't stingy with my money. It's just the principle you know.

Me: I want to breastfeed off your mother.

Some Random Asshole: You can't tell me you can't go out there and get a job. There's jobs open everywhere, and this lazy bitch can't even find one but has 7 kids, I mean you tell me what's wrong with that picture?

Me: There's a Zebra in my ass.

Some Random Asshole: Either way if the baby is mine, I'll be a good dad to it. I don't know if me and her will work out but dammit Imma be a good dad.

Bartender: LAST CALL!

Don't get me wrong. There are people I do want to see, to talk too. Friends. People I haven't seen in a while. Fun people. Just not Toenail people. I think that's what I'm going to start referring to them as: Toenail people.

THE DAY I MET A SCHIZOPHRENIC

One day I was in my room watching the movie Terminator Genisys illegally, and I'm glad I did. That movie sucked. And there's a knock at the door. A strange knock, if that makes sense. I know how every single one of my friends knock on my door. How my mother knocks. This knock didn't sound like any of them. I go answer and there's this very skinny, older woman with little teeth standing there smoking a cigarette. Gray tank top, pink sweatpants.

She goes, "Hi my name is (I honestly don't remember, you'll understand why), I'm Butch's wife. He has a son named Blue and I was told Blue might be here. Is he here?"

I go "Um, no. I've never heard of him, and the only people here are me and my roommate."

She immediately changes subjects and goes "I'm a big fan of glass partisan shops and stores and I absolutely love your door. Did you do that?" referring to this sticker on my door that says "Welcome: You're here to be part of our family."

I go, "No, I didn't do that. My ex-girlfriend put that on there."

She replies with, "Ex-girlfriend huh? Yeah, shit happens." Okay.

Now here's where it gets crazy. She changes subjects again and opens with, "I'm not high on dope. I'm a diagnosed bipolar schizophrenic." You just changed the mood from bad to worst. That's like saying, "Don't worry, I'm not carrying any knives, but I didn bring my bazooka!"
She continues, "I've been off my medicine for 11 days. I was supposed to go to get Xanax two days ago but my husband beat the shit out of me and I wasn't able to get an appointment because I didn't want anybody to know that he beats me. Being bipolar, it makes your emotions do like this" and she starts raising her hand up and down like she's raising the roof.

At this point, since I'm standing there with the door open, my cat Max runs out of the house. She sees Max go out the door and says, "Is that a cat?"

Is that a cat?! What do you think it is? No, it's a fucking lizard.

I said "Yeah, that's a cat. His name is Max" and I'm really trying not to laugh in her face now. She's on Mars right now obviously. Then she goes "How much do those go for?" Seriously, what the fuck does that even mean? Is she plotting to take my cat to the pawn shop? Like, I can see her developing a cat-napping plot in her head as she's asking me this. I tell her, "I don't remember but I got him from the animal shelter."

Then she goes "Well, whenever Blue gets here, just have him give me or his daddy a call" completely forgetting that I just told her I don't know who in the hell Blue is. So, I just said, "Okay, I will" and I shit you not, she just stands there looking at me.

Now, part of me is really feeling bad for her. Even if she's lying about everything else, she's obviously on dope or some brain-altering substance and looking for a score of any kind. She's so desperate, she's obviously going door-to-door looking for any drug she can get her hands on. And again, she's just standing there with her cigarette looking at me with the thousand-yard stare. So now, I'm thinking she wants me to give her drugs or money, that's what this is. She's about to proposition me for sex in exchange for said drugs/money. Then she goes "It sure is hot out here, you know?" So now, I'm thinking, she wants to come inside.

Now, I really consider myself to be a kind person. However, I'm not about to let an admitted dope-using, bipolar, schizophrenic, memory-losing, Xanax-taking, person who gets beat up by her husband into my house. I know. Rude, right? Call me crazy. So, I said "Well, you can't come inside but I can give you a bottle of water." And she goes "No, that's okay, thank you, God bless you, love your door" and just turns around and starts walking down the road. Like we didn't just have a really fucked up conversation. I watched her out my window to see if she was literally going door-to-door looking to score something but no, she kept walking until she was out of my sight.

The very next day, I found out this poor woman was arrested at our local Wal-Mart for harassing customers. Was she? Was she really? Or was she just complementing their doors and cats?

CORONA VIRUS CHALLENGE

We are in the middle of a pandemic so I guess it would be apropos not to dedicate some time to at least part of this book to it. Don't worry though, dear reader. This won't be political. I'm not going to get into conspiracy theories or tell you why or why not you should be vaccinated. Plus, it's a little depressing and I like to keep things upbeat. I do want to tell you about the first time I went to Wal-Mart shortly after the pandemic became noticeably real.

So, this one day I go to Wal-Mart. Now, I'm legit looking for bleach because I recently discovered I have this black mold growing in my refrigerator and I need some bleach. But when I get to Wal-Mart, I discover they are out of it. The back story was as Covid-19 was spreading, it had not hit my home state of Oklahoma yet. But then it did. Oklahoma got its first official case of the corona virus and suddenly, all these anti-vaxxers who were so boisterous on social media suddenly didn't exist anymore. It's real. Oklahoma has it. And as I began walking through Wal-Mart, I began noticing something I had never noticed before. It was like there was some sort of new TikTok challenge going on where you must Clorox wipe your bread, bleach your ham, Draino your cheese. No mayo! Instead, baking soda. Every single chemical related to cleaning had vanished, like a shitty episode of the Twilight Zone.

It reminded me a bit of Y2K. I lived through what would be known as the lamest apocalypse in history of the world. For those of you too young to remember, Y2K was a computer bug that was set to crash the world and send us all into darkness. When complex computer programs were first written in the 1960s, engineers used a two-digit code for the year, leaving out the "19." So, 1962 was just "62." As the years went on and the year 2000 was fast approaching, many believed that the systems would not interpret the "00" correctly, therefore causing a major glitch in the system and crashing computers all around the world. People thought planes would drop out of the sky. Nuclear missiles would be launched. People bought bomb shelters and stocked up on food, gas and funs. You couldn't find a battery of any kind to save your life.

And then, on January 1st, 2000, Americans watched on their TVs as footage was shown of the rest of the world partying their asses off and absolutely nothing happening. No mass black outs. No riots. Just people partying. Now paranoid Grandpa Joe has a bomb shelter full of Double A's.

Same thing on December 21, 2012. Supposedly, that was the last day written on the Ancient Mayans calendar and many people believed it would be the end of the world. Many not realizing that leap years exist and that ancient cultures can't predict the future because they're not magical. Regardless, people were watching cameras of other places around the world to see if anything crazy was happening. Were Aliens in spaceships just outside of Earth's orbit? Were people being sucked up into the sky? Was Jesus coming back so we could party with him on his birthday for days later? No one knew. And as climatic as a popcorn fart, nothing happened. Cult leaders were made into liars. People who stocked up on food now had no idea what to do with 6,000 cans of beans. It was embarrassing.

It makes you wonder what happened to us as a race. Where's the toughness? Our ancestors would be rolling over in their graves if they saw us now. Back in the day, they didn't have bleach. They didn't have Clorox wipes. Nobody panicked and bought all the toilet paper they could. Mainly because they didn't have toilet paper then, but you get my point. If your sandwich had a rat turd on it, you didn't wipe it off. No, you ate the rat turd sandwich like a man. If you got bit by a diseased flea, you took a nice, creamy shit the next day into a bucket and tossed it out of your living room window like a gentleman. Then, you and all your Bubonic plague buddies died, and you were buried and burned in mass graves. Tough.

Nowadays, we're filling our bathtubs with hand-sanitizer and carrying bleach on us like its pepper spray. As soon as a stranger even coughs in the same restaurant as you, you throw bleach in their eyes and shout, "Be gone, shit demon!" I don't know if the Corona Virus makes you poop, I haven't looked up the symptoms, but all the good viruses and diseases do. I'm assuming this one does. Ebola. E. Coli. Bubonic plague. Dysentery. Late night Taco Bell the next morning after a heavy night of drinking. They all do it.

Basically, what I'm saying is, this is how cults start. Soon we're going to be a nation of people wearing togas made from stitched together Clorox wipes. We'll start naming our children what we think are important names like "Windex" or "OxiClean Bartholemule Davis, Jr." Old men in the future will tell stories like, "Before the government dropped a nuclear bomb on the UnWashed in 2032, there was so much soap. Prisoners in jail would sculpt chess pieces out of it. It was so abundant. We used to mindlessly throw away things people are killed for now, like sponges."

I'm not sure what I'm even talking about anymore. Let's move on.

NIGHT OF THE SINGING GIRL

This is the story of a super awkward moment that happened to me one night at work.

So, at the time, my job title was Catering Supervisor. I worked for a company called Sodexo who was hired by our local university. I did caterings for weddings, proms, town meetings, almost anything you can think of. So, this one time, I was at work, cleaning up after this catering and I feel this arm come around me. It was this student, a girl. Not to be mean, seriously, this student was a nice girl. However, she was kind of known to be a little touched in the head, if that makes sense. A little off. Her medicine tablet is short on pills if you know what I mean.

This girl puts her arm around me and goes, "Hey what's up" and we make small talk for a minute. She brings up the fact that she's excited for a Karaoke Night coming up soon at the college. I'm like, "Oh yeah, that's cool. What are you singing?" She goes blah blah blah by blah blah (I don't remember who it was, never heard of the artist/song before.) So, I go "Oh I've never heard that." She pulls out her phone, goes to YouTube and looks up the song. I hate when people do this by the way. Very rarely does someone pull out their phone, which has a nice volume, nothing else around you is distracting you, and you hear a song you like. But whatever, I'm nice. So, I listen. She says, "I really like this song cause I can match the tone perfectly" and she starts singing the song.

Now, she's not looking down, or up, or away as she's singing the song. She's looking at me, making direct eye contact, singing the song. I don't remember all the lyrics, but her face starts matching the expressions in the song. Some girl whose heart was broken and "how could you do this to me" and she's making like these angry faces at me. Like, she's not singing for me, she's singing at me. Like I was the asshole who broke her heart. I start to feel uncomfortable, so I interrupt her and say, "She sounds like Emma Watson." Nothing. She doesn't even acknowledge what I just said. She just keeps looking at me with an angry face singing this heart break song. People are starting to notice what's going on. People are walking behind her and looking at us with confused looks on their faces. Like they're thinking, "Did that guy just break up with her? What an asshole." Or, "Is she serenading him?" She is not stopping.

So, I interrupt her again and just go, "Oh, nice" with that fake complement voice, which didn't work. The fake complement voice only amplified her face and singing. Direct, intense eye contact. I'm like awkwardly looking away, trying to find some means of escape without being rude. "Please God, someone save me." You could've run up and kicked me in the nuts at that very moment and I would've been like, "Oh God thank you. Thank you so much for kicking me where it hurts the most."

And then it hits me.

"Oh no, she's not going to stop." I look down at her phone at that little red bar Youtube has on their videos. "She's going to sing all 4 minutes of this song with people surrounding us." I didn't know what to do. I thought about Homer-Simpsoning it and just slowly start backing away into a bush and disappear forever. Or maybe throwing my shoe with a "Look over there!" and run away.

Finally, I'm like "Cool, well I got to get back to work, I'll see you around" ... and she still doesn't stop.

So, I just start walking away as if she's not there. An as I'm walking away, she keeps going. I can feel her glaring at the back of my head with this, "You son of a bitch!" look on her face even though I didn't do anything. As I'm walking away, I hear her sing the lyrics, "How could you, How could you do this to me," and I can feel all these eyes on me and I just start booking it. Walking fast like a mugger is walking behind me. I get back behind the door, close it, and I'm like "What the hell was that about? Did I wrong this person?"

Long story short, I will not be attending karaoke night. I can just see it now. She's going to get on stage with a Power Point presentation with pictures of me and a laser pointer, singing this song and pointing me out in the crowd. The crowd will start booing me and throw tomatoes at me. No thank you to that.

My Trip to The Eye Doctor

I went to the eye doctor today and remembered exactly why I hate going to the eye doctor. Don't get me wrong, both places in town have extremely nice employees, but the actual tests are just two hours of hell to the point where you're like "Ya know what? I think I'll just be blind. Use some Tabasco sauce as eye drops."

First, there's the pre-torture before the main event. They sit you down in this chair and they're like "Okay Daven we're going to shoot these air bullets into both of your eyes. Go ahead and stare at this laser." And if you flinch too much, they have to do it again like an MRI machine. MREye? I know because I did so and the nurse laughed at me. I had to be shot in the eye three times. So, bonus. Then they spin this automated table around like it was made for Dr. Evil to the next torture device. Then they're like "Okay go ahead and stare at this second laser and ignore everything you've ever heard about staring directly into lasers."

Once you've finished appetizers then it's on to the main course. They make you take your contacts out so your world is just a colorful blur. And they're like "Okay Dolphin follow me" and you're a 34 old man so you can't ask "Will you hold my hand please? Or maybe I can just grab the back of your shirt, so I don't get lost?" How do they resist the urge to walk away really fast just to mess with the patients? Leave them there in the middle of the hallway alone like "Hello? A-Anyone here? I don't know where I am, and you guys made me throw my vision in the trash can... Marco?!"

They sit you down in an isolated tiny room and you can hear the doctor in the next room talking to a patient, "Number 1 or number 2? Is this better or worse? Number 3... Number 4? So you from Oklahoma? Number 5... Number 6? What kind of a dog you have?" And I'm freaking out cause I'm not sure if my birthplace or owning a dog is vital to my eye prescription. Doctor finally comes in and basically goes "I'm going to shine this light in your eye. Then I'm going to shine that light into your eye. Then this really bright helmet light as close to your eye as possible as you try to stare at lights on the ceiling. Again, forget everything they've ever told you about staring at lasers or the Sun." Then he grabs this Men In Black memory eraser and leans in way to close to your face. My beard touched his beard. Men's beards should never touch. You're like, "Is this dude trying to make out with me? Do I get a discount for doing that cause this is going to be expensive? I don't have insurance. I can't even tell what he looks like." And he shines that thing into both your eyes for 10 minutes while you're struggling to keep them open. You're kicking your feet and hitting the seat like an Alien is about to burst through your abdomen and he's 2 centimeters from your face going, "So how's work been going?"

I guess they only had one doctor on today because at the end of my exam they dilated my eyes and the doctor said, "I'll be back shortly." "Shortly" ended up being about forty minutes so when he came back, they had to dilate my eyes again.

Where I live, they do this thing every December called The Festival of Light(s). (Everyone says "lights" but it's actually the Festival Of Light, as in the light of the Lord and savior Jesus of Nazareth, as my boss was once told by an angry customer.) Let me tell you, when your eyes have been dilated twice and you drive by the Festival of Lights, let's just say it reminded me of college. I think I actually saw the Lord, it was so bright and beautiful. Followed by this river of red taillights going down the road. I could taste colors.

So basically I was tortured for 2 hours and had to pay them money for it. Say thank you. Then they send you down the road on a mushroom adventure.

4 Stars on Yelp. Would've given 5 but no one offered me a lollipop. Will return. I must. I have to get my glasses in a week.

The Gas Station Employee

Remember earlier when I was telling you about Toenail People? You ever been going about your day. Running chores. Paying bills. And during this, you run into a stranger that just downloads their sad life problems into their brain. This is that story.

When I originally told this story, I typed "I'm not going to name the classy establishment I was at to avoid embarrassment (on their behalf) and possible firings" but now that I'm publishing this book, it was at my local Valaro, which if you don't have one in your part of the town, it's a gas station. I walk in to buy said Gatorade and the gentleman currently running the shift of this florid building greets me. I don't know this man. I have never seen this man before. He greets me as a customer...

"HEY MAN! (a bit aggressive) How you doin'?"

"I'm alright man. How are you?"

"Slowly dying inside."

Hah, a joke. I enjoy playful banter and pithy quips. So I respond...

"Same man, same. At least we're dying toge-"

And the guy interrupts me and just goes off. He just starts telling me every problem he has in the world. Goddamn it! It's happening again!

"Yeah, my wife just up and took my kids to Alabama and she has no right to do that ya know cause I'm 80% sure the little bastards are mine and if she wants to lawyer up I'll get a DNA test right now. I'm making nine dollars an hour now and the manager already promised me as soon as he gets someone hired I'm getting promoted to manager and hell that's ten an hour right there guaranteed. You can't just run off with some guy you met in Muguskee, Mugee, M'Skogee..."

"Muskogee?"

"Yeah Muskgeegee ain't nothing there but lowlifes anyway so shit man."

Believe it or not I'm paraphrasing because he said a lot more than what I wrote. You're welcome. I tried to be nice and sympathetic towards the guy. Obviously, this dude has some things on his mind and maybe I am the only person he can talk to about it. So I say,

"Yeah man, that's crazy. Sorry to hear that brother, really. But she can't just move your kids across the country. That's kidnapping. She would have to have lega-"

"Bullshit I know! Hell, I'm getting a car soon no more bike or catching rides ya know hehehe. She ain't happy with the life I can provide for her she can fuck right off ya know, ain't no sweat off my back. Hell, I'll be manager soon."

Again, as I stated earlier. These people don't want your advice or sympathy. They just want to talk through you, around you, not to you. They want to lie to themselves out loud so that if maybe you believe it, they can believe it too.

At this point, I just tried to end it.

"Yeah man, yeah. That's... how much for this Gatorade?" So, I can run out this store and away from your depressing life and half unfinished skull tattoo on your forearm. I'm telling you people; this seems to happen to me *a lot* in life. I can't just have a simple, "Hi how are you" transaction. People have this burning desire to tell total strangers their life secrets.

Now I have to walk around with the knowledge that this guy's dream of managing for $9.00 an hour to afford a car and a DNA test to prove this eighty percent sure theory the kids his wife just kidnapped to Alabama are his. Now I'll never know how the story ended. I inadvertently just watched a whole season of "This Dude's Life Sucks Hard" and left it on a cliffhanger I'll never finish. Bullshit.

It makes me want to go back three months from now when he's forgotten all about me, burst into the store, "HEY MAN! Are the kids yours? Is your wife dead? Did you get a car? How's management and what are your plans to improve morale around this bitch?" Just to either get the answers I want or watch the horror and confusion on his face when I bombard him with questions about his shitty life. I'm pulling for you though, Half-Skull-On-Forearm guy.

The Day from Hell At Work

Guys, I'm having a really bad day. Can I tell you how my day started today?

It started when I woke up and, you ever wake up and see how bright it is outside and you're like "That's way too bright outside for it be 9:00 AM." Sure enough, I pick up my phone to see what time it is and it won't cut on. My phones dead. The charger wasn't plugged in all the way so it died in the middle of the night. And you get that thought instantly in your brain and the camera zooms into your face...

"Oh shit! I'm late for work!"

And what's even worse I didn't know how late I was. I go and look at my computer and I'm currently 12 minutes late. I'm running around my house, one leg in the pants, trying to wipe the sleep crust out of my eye, looking for my shoes, keys, wallet, my sanity. As I'm in the bathroom getting ready, I hear my front door. Someone's beating on my door.

Now I live right down the road from my job, so my boss and coworkers have no problem driving to my house and waking me up. I'm not allowed sick days. They're just like "Put on this hazmat suit and work that double." I answer the door and it's one of my bosses and I'm like, "I know! I'm sorry! I'm coming!" And she goes "Well just so you know [an employee] had to leave so you're not in the dish room, you're cooking in Dusty's." Okay cool fine no problem.

I go upstairs to Dusty's and there's nothing. I mean nothing. No tomatoes, no onions, no ham, no buns, no fries, just barren, plastic containers as far as the eye can see, and I have about 4 minutes to get everything I need to open Dusty's. I can already see a line of customers forming. So I run downstairs and I'm grabbing everything I can think of: ice, bread, buns, a spatula, stuff I'm not even sure I need, stuff I never need, just grab grab grab grab.

Here's where it goes bad.

I open the door to Dusty's and students start pouring in. To save me a little time, I throw like 11 burgers on the grill because that's mainly what students order. Now, because I was running around, late for work, trying to scavenge anything to help me, I didn't notice that the crew the night before had cleaned the bar grill. And when you clean it, all this grease and 'gunk' builds up on this tray.

So I'm swiping all these students cards one by one by one and I start to smell "burning". I turn around and see these abnormal Devil flames and black smoke rising from my grill like the pit of Hades. So again, "Oh shit!", so I go over and turn the grill off but it was too late. The oily gunk on the tray was on fire and it wasn't going out.

And then...

The fire alarm goes off, and it's so loud. And I'm so stressed and frustrated and late for work and there's nothing stocked in Dusty's and me and my girl broke up recently and the students are looking at me with fear and panic in their eyes...and I just start laughing. Uncontrollable, gut-busting belly laughter. It's like all this stress and anger inside me just erupted into a volcano of laughing.

Then, the alarm goes off again. And I start laughing even harder. I can't move. I'm paralyzed with laughter. It quickly goes off, it was only on for a second, and then...

Once again, the alarm goes off again.

I have tears down my face. I'm trying so hard to stop laughing, it's making it worse. My jaw muscles start hurting. My world is on fire and I'm laughing like a complete lunatic. The alarm ended up going off 4 or 5 times in total. But eventually, it was over. The alarm stayed off. I was able to compose myself. I start to clean up. An employee buddy of mine comes upstairs and I say, "So were you guys busy downstairs?" He goes, "Well... we were. But when the fire alarms went off, all the students evacuated the building."

And I just lost it, I started laughing again because all the students in the cafe left, and every single student in Dusty's, the origin of the fire alarm, stayed. Not only stayed, but more showed up as if to say, "If I'm gonna burn alive, I'm gonna be full when I do it."

That's how my day started, and I work a double. I had a coworker ask me if I would work Dusty's for him tonight and I almost responded by jumping out the 3rd story windows, just to make sure he knew I meant it when I said, "No."

SHOW ME YOUR BUTTHOLE

I was at work the other day and had a friend tell me she was annoyed. When I asked why, she gave me a very strange answer. I'm not going to mention her name here, hey Hanna, but I assure you she exists. But she said...

"My boyfriend won't let me look at his butthole."

"...What?" Of all the problems in life, ya know?

"He won't let me look at his butthole. Like, 'Really dude? Not even a glance.'"

Ladies, you must understand something. When we date you, we have to salvage any shred of sexiness we can. We'll give you pieces of our true self over time but it's hard to hang on to sexy when you've been dating someone for a while. Because one day you're just like, "Screw it" and you just decide to fart right in front of her. And your fart smells like a dead rhino. Negative one sexy point. Then she finds out you have a special toe knife you use to prevent hemmotarded ingrown toenail syndrome." Negative one sexy point. Then she finds out you wear the same underwear nine days in a row. Negative one sexy point. Then you get an ass cramp in the middle of sex and your dick goes limp so you all your mom and cry about it to her. Negative seven thousand sexy points.

Father Time is a bitch, and he will reveal to you ladies all the unsexiness (Is that a word?) we've been trying to hide from you for weeks, months, even years. This girl I use to date, she would come into the bathroom when I was pooping. There I was, pale, hairy thighs glistening in the bathroom light. It smelled like who-done-it-and-what-for. And she would want to talk while I was gently trying to squeeze out an avalanche of yesterday's Taco Bell without it sounding like a whistling mouse or aggressively stirred up spaghetti.

"Will you please leave because I would like to have sex with you again one day and I don't exactly feel like this is the image of me I want in your head before asking, nay, begging as I'm sure I will now have to do."

I know you couples out there know what I'm talking about. I bet you're reading this and looking over at your man as he's playing video games in his underwear with Dorito crumbs stuck in his belly hair. No one has ever said, "Remember that time I could hear you shitting from the living room, and I got super horny." That's never happened. Maybe in Germany it's happened but it's a super rarity here in America.

So please, please, just let us have our quarter-sized butthole to hide from you. That's all we ask, but a quarter. So, we can both pretend I'm Game of Thrones Jason Mamoa during sexy time.

That time I Shit Myself

We've all done it. Since birth. It's something no human has ever been able to escape from. At some point in our life, there will be a time, when you defecate on yourself. May be an untrustworthy fart or a brutal sneeze during food poisoning. Sooner or later, it will find you. It found me. Here's my story.

I was at this local restaurant in my hometown called Mama Carol's, having lunch with a friend, and all of a sudden it felt like an anvil dropped in my stomach. It became heavy very quickly. I lost my appetite. Then I could feel my stomach expand and it hit me...

"I need to get out of here right now. I have to shit."

It was so sudden. Out of nowhere, like the waiter put Ex-lax in my tea or something. Going from a calm lunch to anxiety-ridden stomach pains is an emotional roller coaster. I pull out my wallet and just threw money on the table. I could've given the waitress a $100 bill for all I know. I speed-walk outside which makes me look like I was walking out on my bill. As soon as I get to my car door, I drop my keys. My stomach rewards me for that with an inside gut punch. Like a quick jab of pain. I get into the car, speed off towards Sonic where I encountered the longest red light of my entire life. It was like watching an elderly woman cross the road who didn't have legs and her leg nubs had gorilla glue on them. I'm shaking the steering wheel. I'm sweating. I'm cursing the red light.

"HURRY UP YOU DICKHOLE RED LIGHT! HURRY! I HATE YOU!"

I turn down the street and get behind a black Honda whose license plate I memorized just in case they were going so slow I thought about reporting a crime and nailing their car as the culprit but that's, you know, illegal.

At this point my stomach is telling me, "Hey guy... maybe 2 minutes. Tops." I'm yelling at the Honda while cursing the Gods. I'm looking around for churches, businesses, anything that might be open and have a bathroom. There's nothing. Just a giant neighborhood of houses. I actually thought about jumping out of the car and banging on someone's door like in a horror movie. Like I'm being chased by Jason Voorhees.

"Help! Please! Let me in! It's coming!"

And God bless anyone that would let a stranger shit in their house. You would have to tip them, right? "Hey man, here's a $20. I got a little on the seat. That's my bad. Might want to bleach that. You have a lovely home." Send them a Christmas card every year maybe.

"Honey, who sent us this Christmas card?"

"That's the guy who ran in our house and shit on our floor!"

The pain at this point is torturous. I'm crowning. All I hear is this robot voice in my head: "Warning. Warning. You have 30 seconds to evacuate. Warning. Warning. Prepare for evacuation." Usually, I'm the polite driver at four-way stops. I'll gently wave you by. Not today, asshole. My forehead is damp with sweat now. My body is hot to the touch. I pull into my driveway. By the way, your stomach knows when you got to have to shit. I don't know the science behind it, but I know every time I pull into my driveway, and I have to shit, your body is like, "Oh good, he's home everyone. Push harder. He'll appreciate us more." I get inside my house and am greeted by my two cats. They see me heading towards the kitchen, so they run to the kitchen because they think they're about to get food. They're about to get shit on if they don't move. I do this, like, "dance-walk" like I'm jumping off hot coals trying to avoid my asshole cats and that's when... a little bit happened.

It was just a little bit. A classy bit. Like if you were at a party and that amount came out, you would be like, "I can hang out for like 30 more minutes. No one will know. But after that I got to go home. I'm an adult. I pay bills. I am better than this."

I get to my bathroom, sit down on the toilet, I let Jesus take the wheel. The angels were singing. There's deer joyfully galloping through golden fields of wheat. Emotionally, I am swimming in a giant pool of Cinnamon Toast Crunch. The relief was beautiful.

And that's when I looked around and saw the brown roll of (no) toilet paper staring back at me on the floor like, "Yeah. You deserve this. Bet you won't put off going to the store to get toilet paper again, will you?" All the roll had on it was those three glue rings this pathetic scrap of toilet paper hanging off it. I look in the bottom cabinet and I see some drain-o and cotton swabs for ear cleaning. I wonder how many cotton swabs... never mind.

You don't need to know the rest of the story because I don't like to tell personal stories about myself. But just know it had a happy ending. So now, time to go to Walmart for some good ol' fashion toilet paper.

And socks.

I'M BLEEDING FROM MY TESTICLES

On this particular morning I woke up because I had to pee. The second I stood up out of bed, raging agony bit me on the inner thigh. It was instantaneous pain. It stung and burned at the same time. I go to the bathroom, pull my undies down, and as soon as I do, a trail of blood begins running down my leg all the way to my ankle. I thought, "Hm, might want to have a doctor glance at that."

You really take for granted mundane things in life when you're not in pain. Putting on my shoes was grim torment. I limp to the car and off to Healthcare Stat I go. Remind me to write a letter to city council about the potholes in this town. I felt every tortuous pothole. Every bump. Every slope. Every uneven street was a quick reminder that life sucks right now.

I get to HealthCare Stat. I pay $95.00. The nurse sees me. After explaining I'm bleeding from what I think is my testicles or thigh, I'm not sure, I tell them straight up, "I am not a drug seeker, but every single step burns with pain. I want real pain medicine when I'm done please because I know this is going to hurt long after you're done." She informs me by law she is not allowed to prescribe narcotics since she is a nurse practitioner. She says, "The most I can give you is Tylenol-3." Great. Do I get a lollipop too? Will you also kiss da booboo? So, I'm like fuck that, thank you very much. Do I get my $95.00 back since you did nothing and saw me naked? No? Cool. I limp back to my car and that's when I noticed there is blood on my driver seat. Three quarter-sized puddles soaked. Do you know how much blood you have to bleed for it to go through your underwear, through your pants, to become visible on car seats? Women reading this right now are like, "Yeah, we do know, asshole." Whatever amount I was bleeding was the correct amount.

I get back in my car and every time I hit a speed bump, I cuss out the universe. I must've looked like a mad man. I pull into my local hospital which, by the way, super smooth parking lot. Two big thumbs up on the pavement job. I get out and start penguin-walking to the door. I go in, not one person in the lobby. Yes! I'm sure it would be a little off putting to see a man with blood stains on his crotch walking into a hospital. You'd be like, "Yep. I know why he's here. Got his dick stuck in the toaster. Been there." A nurse asked what seems to be the issue? I opened with, "I'm dripping blood on your floor right now." I didn't mean for it to sound as ominous as it did. As I'm giving her my information, I notice blood dripping on her floor.

At this point, I'm getting a little scared if I'm being honest. I'm not a doctor but I know I shouldn't be bleeding this much from what's not a gunshot wound. The doctors are nice. I tell him I've bled a lot today. I told them I went to HealthCare Stat and left because they said they couldn't prescribe me pain meds I wanted. "Again, I'm not a drug seeker, but I want the good stuff." They tell me to put on a gown. I go to their bathroom; I take my pants off and I was taken aback when I saw my inner right leg was crimson red. It was so unsettling to see how much blood there was. I had been bleeding out since that first moment I used the bathroom this morning. I come out of the bathroom. They ask me to lay down. They lift up my gown and now a total of six people in my town today have seen my cash and prizes, so, awesome. You are welcome. It's not a lot of cash and prize either when you're bleeding near the area. Three dollars and twelve cents maybe. The guy is moving and swatting my balls like a cat does a cat toy. I'm like "Jesus dude! They're not just for show ya know." Then he tells me...

You ready for this?

"Mr Davis, it looks like you have an infected abscess in the crevice between your genitals and thigh." He looks at the nurse, "Go get an IND kit and 1% lidocaine." I go, "What's an IND kit?" He goes, "IND means Incision and Drainage. You're bleeding out because the infected area is trying to clean itself. We're going to cut it open and drain any remaining pus and blood to give you relief."

I'm sorry, what now?

You're going to take a scalpel near my nut sack? That's pretty much all I heard. Show me your hands, Doc. How steady are you? Ask the nurse if she knows the chances of an Earthquake today? I want the facts.

Then he goes, "Now Mr. Davis, you're going to feel some pressure." For those who've never experienced pressure, let me tell you, pressure feels exactly like a fire needle.

I've had kidney stones, broken fingers, tattoos in painful places, but when he stuck that fire needle in that infected abscess, I about kicked the nurse in her stupid face. I had never felt pain like that. I was banging my head against the pillow. My teeth were breaking on each other. I was motherfucking the Doctor's family and ancestors and his cavemen uncles. I have never experienced pain like that. It consumes your mind. It's all you see, hear, taste, feel. He did it four times. Injected me four times with lidocaine. Right when he's done, "Okay, buddy, here we go."

Please, please, just kill me. He's *squeeeeeezing* this thing, and *squeeeezing*. Not gonna lie, almost shit myself (again). Wouldn't have cared either. I would've grabbed it and attacked him like a monkey just as long as he let me go.

Squeeeeeze. Squeeeeze.

At one point, I hear this audible "pop." I look down and I see a spattering of pus and blood flying through the air. This poor guy had it on his forearm. You know, we all think we've had bad days, but you ever had to squeeze out the pus and blood near someone's genitals before lunch? Might as well just go back to bed and start your day over. This guy is hitting it in every direction, getting every drop out as I'm grasping the bed rails. Despite the pain, I can honestly say I didn't cry. Probably because I was so dehydrated from blood loss and my body was saving every liquid it had left.

"Okay buddy, we're done. You can relax." "Relax," you say? Surrrre. I'll just act like I wasn't just tortured in an Iraqi war camp, you sadist. We conversate for a minute and he asks where I work? I tell him. He asks if I walk a lot. I'm like "Oh yeah, about 10 hours a day." He goes, "Well you need to walk as little as possible, keep the area clean and dry. Change your gauze at least 3 times a day. You may still experience drainage."

Just give it to me straight, Doc. How long do I have?

I get up to get dressed and, have I stressed enough about the amount of my own blood I've seen today? But I can walk without pain. Thank you, lidocaine! He also prescribed me hydrocodone which 10/10, definitely recommend. I'd like to meet the dudes that invented lidocaine and hydrocodone and buy them a beer.

I spent the rest of the day drugged up. Still draining. Afraid to sneeze. Afraid to move. Still in pain.

At least I got the day off.

Printed in Great Britain
by Amazon